Conjugal Visits In Prison

Conjugal Visits in Prison

Psychological and Social Consequences

Jules Quentin Burstein

Lexington Books
D.C. Heath and Company
Lexington, Massachusetts
Toronto

Library of Congress Cataloging in Publication Data

Burstein, Jules.
    Conjugal visits in prison.

    Includes bibliographical references and index.
    1. Prisons—Visits and correspondence with inmates. 2. Soledad
Correctional Training Facility. I. Title.
HV8884.B87   365'.6   76-50485
ISBN 0-669-01287-4

Published simultaneously in Canada

Printed in the United States of America

International Standard Book Number: 0-669-01287-4

Library of Congress Catalog Card Number: 76-50485

To Linda

who circled me with a soft web of tenderness when I needed
it most

and

for my mother and father . . .
who taught me that courage and endurance exist even in the
humblest of lives.

Contents

List of Tables

Acknowledgments

I am grateful for the continuing support and encouragement of several colleagues, and most especially to David Frey who drew out and fostered my creative instincts, to Louis Everstine who tended diligently to the trees while I plowed through the forest, and to Richard Hongisto, sheriff of San Francisco, for his constructive suggestions and critical evaluation.

Special thanks are due to the following personnel at the Soledad Correctional Training Facility, without whose cooperation this study could not have been written: Tom Stone, superintendent, who provided comprehensive staff assistance throughout; E. A. Peterson, associate superintendent, whose ceaseless energy on my behalf preserved my sanity during the rough times; Derral Byers, lieutenant, a most helpful guide in the early days; Leah Bradshaw, correctional counselor; and to all the men at South and Central Facilities who were willing to share the intimacies of their most desperate and hopeful moments.

Finally, my deep and heartfelt appreciation to Dan and Sharon Stathos, who "opened their home" at Soledad to me.

Conjugal Visits In Prison

1 Introduction

The degree of civilization in a society can be judged by entering its prisons.
                                                                —Dostoyevsky

Overview

This book represents the first effort to evaluate the impact of conjugal visits on prisoners at the Correctional Training Facility for men in Soledad, California. To date, it is only the second research project of its kind ever conducted. A phenomenological approach will be used to assess the global meaning of such visits in the total experience of criminal confinement. "Phenomenological," in this context, is used to suggest that the subjects' descriptions of their inner states will be allowed to speak for themselves, without interposing some method of causal explanation. In addition, and more specifically, a study will be made of the relationship between participation in the conjugal visiting program, on the one hand, and marital stability and postparole success factors on the other.

The general strategy of this research was to contrast the differential outcomes of an experimental group of inmates who received conjugal visits with a comparative group whose wives were permitted only regular visits. The study began in May 1975. Final data were collected in May 1976.

From May through early July 1975, structured interviews were conducted in various sectors of the penitentiary among 40 inmates. These were totally confidential in nature as no third party was ever present, and none but the investigator had access to the particular responses of any individual prisoner. Administrative officials at Soledad were totally scrupulous in this regard, with the superintendent of the facility urging all relevant personnel to provide whatever assistance the researcher requested. The superintendent and personnel coordinating the family visiting program asked only that a copy of the findings be made available to them.

Background of the Problem

Deprivation of "normal" sexual outlets in prison has historically been justified as part of the punishment rationale in American penology. The absence of any opportunity for heterosexual relations typically results in a high incidence of

1

homosexuality which, in turn, is often the cause of quarrels, fights, knifings, and, not infrequently, murder. Many inmates who engage in homosexual acts do so not because of their ordinary sexual orientation, but because of frustration and long accumulations of sexual energy. Those who view such behavior as pathological miss the crucial fact that an individual's sex life is not isolated from the entire fabric of his interpersonal relationships and their psychological ramifications.

Perhaps the suppression of heterosexual activity is most trying for the married prisoner who receives regular visits from his wife, but with whom his emotional and physical contact is markedly constrained. At present, California and Mississippi are the only two states in this country permitting married inmates conjugal visits. The program in California, for reasons to be discussed later, is unique in the history of American corrections. Since its inception in 1969, such visits have been little publicized and less studied. In a very real sense, these two isolated programs probably reflect the most straightforward and sensible attempt to humanize the lives of men living under conditions of severe deprivation.

Psychologically, the most apparent fact of imprisonment is the stark reduction in individual autonomy imposed upon the prisoner. All those experiences that facilitate a sense of being able to create one's own world are lost. Time, space, and choice are dramatically telescoped. Henceforth, every moment of every day will be planned in accordance with some dull and monotonous administrative routine, a routine in which the times for eating, showering, watching TV, and lights out will never vary. The space one will be able to move through is bounded by a finite number of square feet extending from one's cell to the mess hall and exercise yard. What kinds of clothes one has, the food one eats, and the books one reads will all be selected and circumscribed by other people.

In many ways, the state of involuntary confinement resembles that of subjects in sensory deprivation experiments. But human beings need stimulation in order to function in a healthy fashion. The systematic loss of perceptual and emotional stimuli can, and does, lead to fear, anxiety, irritability, paranoia, and, ultimately, varying levels of psychic regression, often including total decompensation and psychosis.

All of the limitations of prison life noted above are compounded by the fact that, sexually, there will be no opportunity for contact with women. Inevitably, the result is compulsive masturbation or guilt-ridden homosexual activity, not to mention the ever-present possibility of sexual assault. Sexual fantasies become rampant, and contraband pornographic literature is jealously guarded. The frustration and collective containment of the sexual energy of thousands of young, virile men must inevitably create a highly charged and perennially tense atmosphere within prison walls.

Statement of the Problem

However strained, diminished, and maddening the conditions of deprived sexual expression are for the prisoner, it is important to bear in mind that he is not the only one affected by his incarceration. Most criminals have at least some family members whose lives, in one way or another, will be touched by having a father, son, or brother who has been stripped of his freedom. It may be, though, that the harshest pain of all is that borne by the wives, especially young wives, of men in prison.

It would seem as if the act of imprisonment carries within it an ironic social contradiction, for while it is society's intention (at least partially) to facilitate an increased sense of social cooperation and to promote the values of the "good" citizen in the prisoner, it does so by maximizing his social isolation. From the first day in prison a man's ties with family and friends are curtailed drastically. The process is often a reciprocal one. The social stigma of arrest and conviction tend to erode the involvement of all but the most loyal allies. Conversely, a number of prisoners tend to initiate a restriction of contact based on their own feelings of shame and guilt. The ultimate consequence is a rapid deterioration of that interpersonal matrix that most of us take for granted as the bedrock foundation of our social existence.

Studies relating the impact of imprisonment to family relationships are virtually nonexistent, considering the voluminous research on prisons and prisoners. Visiting records indicate that there is often a relatively small tight core of friends and relatives who visit in more or less periodic fashion for the first two or three years. A major exception to this pattern is the steady reduction in visits from wives during the second year of confinement (Holt and Miller, 1972). It may seem strange that the most intimate relationship is that which becomes least durable with the passage of time, but the seeds of its more rapid deterioration are inherent in the intensity of the relationship. In the first instance, the degree to which interactions with parents, siblings, and other family members and relatives are affected is minor by contrast with the total rupture, both emotionally and sexually, of the day-to-day contact a man has with his wife. The former are blood relatives for life, whereas a wife always has the option of forming new relationships with other men. Additionally, the most intimate contact a married couple enjoys is precisely that of which they are deprived by his imprisonment. It should not surprise us, then, that the divorce rate among married prisoners during their first few years of confinement increases to a rate significantly higher than that of the general population.

The breakdown of marital stability among married prisoners is not only a personal tragedy, but has social repercussions as well. The wife of a man in prison is in a unique position to provide continued moral support and to assist with postparole plans connected with housing, employment, and money. The extent to which a wife deserts a prisoner during the early part of his term diminishes considerably the probability of a successful adjustment after release.

This book addresses itself to the problem of *an examination of the psychosocial consequences of conjugal visits in prison, particularly as these manifest themselves in the duration and quality of the marriage relationship, and the successful reintegration into society of the prisoner after completion of his sentence.*

The justification for conducting such research may be marshaled from several varied, though related, quarters. On the basest of all levels one may consider the pragmatic question of what public good is presently served by our nation's prisons. One direct method of assessment is that of simple cost effectiveness. A glance at some stark statistics is anything but encouraging. It costs about $15,000 a year to keep a man in prison. With 400,000 men and women in state and federal penitentiaries, we have been spending $6 billion annually to house, feed, and provide custody for those persons. But the cost of keeping the system operating is not the only expenditure. We also pour nearly a billion dollars a year into new prison construction, more than $100 million for job-training programs, and $10 million for therapy programs. Given the continued high rate of recidivism (hovering in most instances between 50-70 percent, what all this adds up to is a gigantic capital outlay with very little profit to show for it (Chaneles, 1975).

The combination of astronomical sums of money being spent, together with the massive waste of human lives behind prison walls, creates a self-sustaining failure system whose internal contradictions are rarely subjected to evaluation and analysis. One of the intentions of this study is to contribute to that analysis and, by doing so, hopefully to focus on some alternatives to the present cycle of conviction-imprisonment-parole-arrest-imprisonment. By comparison to the cost of maintaining a bureaucracy that has demonstrated its almost total ineffectiveness (Bagdikian, 1972; Clark, 1974; Mitford, 1974), the current research has potential value in that it explores a possible change in policy that if adopted, would be of negligible cost. It might also provide a research model for rational decisionmaking and investment choices with regard to correctional policies—a model based more on demonstrable success through precise evaluative criteria, rather than one based on dubious theoretical assumptions.

But that is the least of it. The psychological and social reasons that warrant such research are surely critical. The emotional substratum of those reasons rests in large part on the deep strain of sexual puritanism that still exists in this country. Not only in prisons, but in mental hospitals, nursing homes, halfway houses, and other stigmatized social institutions, the reality of and need for sexual expression are either denied, ignored, or denigrated. With regard to prisons, the denial has been rationalized by tepid liberal apologias or by antiquated notions of moral propriety and political wisdom. One can only imagine the diffuse benefits that might accrue to any number of "total institutions" if conjugal visits in prison were shown to be not only scandal-free but of substantive social and psychological value as well.

In the context of the prison setting, such a finding would have broad ideological implications. At the present time, penologists almost universally subscribe to a "treatment" philosophy, the focal assumption of which is that criminals are psychologically disturbed people who, if subjected to various therapeutic techniques, will experience individual improvement and consequently social rehabilitation. The most chilling aspects of this belief were expressed recently by behavioral psychologist James V. McConnell:

I believe that the day has come when we can combine sensory deprivation with drugs, hypnosis and astute manipulation of reward and punishment to gain almost absolute control over an individual's behavior. It should be possible then to achieve a very rapid and highly effective type of positive brainwashing that would allow us to make dramatic changes in a person's behavior and personality. I foresee the day when we could convert the worst criminal in a matter of a few months—or perhaps even less than that. (McConnell, 1970 pp. 74-75)

Can one read such a statement as anything but a travesty of the supposed healing functions of the professional psychologist? The fact is that such a treatment philosophy legitimizes the most hideous and unbridled control over men's lives possessed by any of society's institutions. And it does so by advancing a series of implicit and unargued assumptions which a large sector of our citizenry accepts as fact. The tacit notion, for example, that criminals are "mentally ill" has been much criticized of late. There has been slow but sure recognition that socioeconomic and political factors must have some relationship to the predominance of lower class, and largely nonwhite, criminals who populate most state prisons.

In addition, the goal of therapeutic rehabilitation presupposes that psychotherapy, even at its most refined and sensitive pitch, can be effective in the midst of an environment characterized by isolation, fear, degradation, and oppression. It is ironic to think that anyone would expect healthy, life-enhancing behaviors to develop in an atmosphere that dulls the senses and dampens the spirit unceasingly.

The study with which this book is concerned represents a radical departure from treatment-philosophy-oriented research as a mainstay of coping with criminality. It suggests, instead, that viewing a prisoner as a "case" or "patient" to be manipulated this way and that in order to maximize behavioral change may be an incredibly expensive exercise in futility. It further hypothesizes that creating the conditions for an extended emotional and sexual experience with an intimate loved one may be a much sounder way to promote lasting behavioral change and resocialization. If that is so, the consequent psychological benefits to the prisoner, together with the social assets of family stability and a decrease in recidivism, would raise some provocative questions about the wisdom of prevailing penal practices.

This research is also timely because the problematic nature of sex in prison has, in recent years, been publicized through the advent of a newly emerging legal dimension. The rationale for legal action is based on inmate contention that the threat of violent sexual assault in many prison settings is constant, and as such violates constitutional safeguards deemed applicable in such situations. The following testimony from a young juvenile offender describes an experience that is more the rule than the exception in many juvenile facilities: "I was sixteen years old. . . six of them held a knife to my throat and raped me even though I begged them not to. When it was over, I went to the bathroom and sat down on the toilet. There was blood. . . I never hurt so bad." (Braswell and De Francis, 1972, p. 173).

An increasing number of class action suits are being brought by inmates not only because of the ever-present possibility of homosexual rape, but also on the grounds that they have a human right to sexual relations with their wives despite their loss of freedom. This is, of course, a novel claim, and one that would have been scoffed at a few short years ago. But perhaps such a change in public consciousness based on moral injunction is not so far-fetched after all.

Consider that before prisons existed in this country (a Quaker-inspired reform begun a mere 200 years ago), punishment for crime took the form of execution, torture, mutilation, and exile. With the passage of time we became more "civilized" and only locked people up, thereby depriving them of their liberty and rendering society safe from their possible subsequent criminal actions. It may be that a parallel, and hopefully more successful, transformation is called for today, one that recognizes the existence of the convicted person as a human being still deserving of certain basic human rights. Foremost among these would be an acknowledgement of the importance of a man's wife, as reflected in the availability of conjugal visits on a regular and frequent schedule. Perhaps such a step would herald a small, but dramatic, shift in the history of penology, a history of massive and continued institutional failure, perplexing even to those whose efforts have been most sincere and humanitarian.

A Word on Terminology

The advent of modern penitentiaries and the emphasis on the "rehabilitation" of criminals has been accompanied by some interesting transformations of language. The brutal and uncaring atmosphere of most prisons has been sanitized by the adoption of a new vocabulary designed to make what is done by fiat and unchecked power seem progressive and therapeutic.

Thus the terms listed on the left, which have the dignity of simple truth about them, have in recent years been replaced by the bureaucratic euphemisms on the right:

prison	correctional facility
guard	corrections officer
prisoner	inmate
"the hole"	adjustment center

warden   superintendent
coerced participation in
    psychological processes   treatment

Because the terms on the right are so pervasive in the literature and have been unconsciously absorbed by this writer during the course of extensive research, they will often be used in the body of this study. Still, the reader is forewarned to bear in mind that "the name is not the thing" was never more true than in the "Alice in Wonderland" world of America's prisons.

2

Review of the Literature

Introduction

The study and the results with which this book concerns itself focus on the psychosocial consequences of conjugal visits in a prison setting. The literature related to this subject is unfortunately and surprisingly sparse. Thus this review will be, if not exhaustive, certainly comprehensive. The intention will be to place the findings of the present research in an historical and social psychological context, one which hopefully will provide a meaningful and relevant framework in which to evaluate its significance and implications.

The initial section will provide a cursory glance at the origin and development of the prison as a peculiarly American institution. This will be followed by an examination of the major findings of the effects of sexual deprivation in prison: i.e., the inevitable homosexuality, and psychological and family repercussions, as well as some recent legal decisions related to its legitimacy. Finally a survey will be made of those writings that specifically address themselves to conjugal visits for men in prison, both in this country and abroad. It is hoped that a literature review that includes references to the disparate fields of psychology, sociology, criminology, history, and law will serve not to artificially fragment the vital questions raised by the current study, but to reflect the assets of fruitful interdisciplinary scholarship. If successful, the reader will experience what follows as a tapestry in which each figure enhances and illuminates the composition as a whole.

The Origin and Development of Prisons

Imprisonment as it exists today is a worse crime than any of those committed by its victims; for no single criminal can be as powerful for evil, or as unrestrained in its exercise, as an organized nation.

—George Bernard Shaw (1946)

The first day I got to Soledad I was walking from the fish tank to the mess hall and this guy comes running down the hall past me, yelling, with a knife sticking out of his back. Man, I was petrified. I thought, what the fuck kind of place is this.

—Soledad inmate (Irwin, 1970)

Every day in the United States approximately 1.3 million human beings are legally locked up (Mitford, 1974, p. 5). These include persons in juvenile detention centers, county jails, an estimated 20,000 in federal penitentiaries, and 200,000 in state prisons (Bagdikian, 1972, p. 10). It's a relatively small number when one considers that of every one hundred major crimes committed, only 1.5 result in someone being arrested, convicted, and ultimately imprisoned (Mitford, 1974, p. 302).

Ostensibly, our criminal justice system has a multifaceted rationale for the public act of imprisonment: punishment, deterrence, social isolation, and rehabilitation. Such terms have a moralistic, liberal flavor to them, but no less than a former U.S. attorney general has remarked that "Prisons are usually little more than places to keep people—warehouses of human degradation. Ninety-five percent of all expenditure in the entire corrections effort of the nation is for custody—iron bars, stone walls, guards. Five percent is for hope—health services, education, development employment skills" (Clark, 1974, p. 193). That prisons succeed in their aim of wreaking vengeance and isolating those select members of a particular social class who break its laws is apparent. Less apparent and much more controversial is whether or not deterrence and rehabilitation can any longer be maintained as realities rather than convenient social myths. The ever-increasing crime rate would appear to make deterrence as successful as it was in Elizabethan times when pickpockets plied their trade at the public execution of their colleagues. And as for "rehabilitation," it seems destined in penology to surpass the metaphor value of "schizophrenia" in psychiatry.

But, how did this peculiar institution develop? Ironically, it was the handiwork of a noble-minded group of Americans, whose own descendants now describe it as a place which "denies autonomy, degrades dignity, impairs or destroys self-reliance, inculcates authoritarian values, minimizes the likelihood of beneficial interaction with one's peers, fractures family ties, destroys the family's economic stability and prejudices the prisoner's future prospects for any improvement in his economic and social status" (American Friends Service Committee, 1971, p. 33). Incredible as it may now seem to us, prison was the brainchild of the Pennsylvania Quakers.

In an age when the "modern" prison is a fundamental fact of our social existence, it is difficult to appreciate what a relatively recent innovation it actually is. Prior to the latter portion of the eighteenth century, prisons were used almost exclusively for pretrial detention purposes or for serving very short county jail terms. The more customary forms of punishment ranged from capital punishment to various forms of mutilation (flogging, dismemberment, etc.), exile, and monetary fines. The stocks of Colonial times were in fact considered a gentle form of punishment whose cornerstone was the supposed humiliation experienced by its sufferer.

In 1787, Benjamin Franklin was host for a meeting of prominent citizens at his home in which the discussion centered on alternatives to then current methods of punishing convicted criminals. Benjamin Rush (sometimes referred to as the American "father of psychiatry") was in attendance and along with other fellow Quakers proposed a radically new approach based on the democratic belief that deviance required reformation as much as vengeance, or indeed as a substitute for vengeance.

The seeds of the rehabilitation philosophy were spawned that day, including proposals for housing classification, prison labor, indeterminate sentences, and "individualized treatment for convicts according to whether crimes arose from passion, habit or temptation" (Killinger and Cromwell, 1973, p. 23). These recommendations had sprung from the Christian belief that prolonged isolation would lead the prisoner to involve himself in prayer, meditation, reflection, and penance.

By 1790, new legislation had been passed in Pennsylvania that provided for the renovation of the Walnut Street Jail, in accordance with this new and "revolutionary" penal advance. Henceforth corporal punishment, mutilation, and degradation were to be abolished, and in fact by 1800 the death penalty became limited to punishment only for murder or treason. By 1796, New York, impressed with a commissioner's report on the Philadelphia system, inaugurated a similar program at Auburn prison. By 1820, almost all of the states had adopted this new model and the contemporary penitentiary was born. Thus began a period of critical change in the last waystation of the criminal justice matrix, not only in the United States, but throughout the world. The nineteenth century saw a prolific expansion of prisons in this country, together with the initiation of prison labor, custody classification, educational and vocational training programs, and parole departments (Killinger and Cromwell, 1973). There was a self-congratulatory air about the new developments, stemming often from authentic humanitarian sentiments as yet untainted by thorny political and social questions. In short, it was a time of optimism that the Quakers fostered, a conviction that the age-old necessity of punishing human beings for transgressing society's rules could be effected by a spirit of charity and concern rather than cruelty and debasement. It was the beginning of a dream that has refused to die.

Now, barely 200 years after its inception, the documented failures of our prison system are legion. No longer enamored by the promise they hold, we search frantically for new ways to sustain them despite our disillusionment and our anger at their obvious failure to secure the social benefits we expected them to yield. Leinwand (1972) has commented on the basic contradiction inherent in the liberal notion of prisons serving simultaneously as agencies of rehabilitation while operating on a foundation in which custodial factors and retributive punishment are administrative priorities. It has been observed that the average guard is paid less than a zookeeper, and that while Delaware spends $13.71 daily for food and custody per prisoner, the comparible figure for Arkansas is $1.55 (Bagdikian, 1972, p. 10-13).

Galtung (1958) has written of prisons not only as the least successful of our social institutions, but also as having an "air of irrelevance" about them. He refers to the psychosocial effects of confinement as generating inevitable frustrations, i.e., the guilt or remorse of being apprehended; the sudden removal from a normal social space to one isolated and claustrophobic; the complete absence of heterosexual relations; and the sustained inability to develop physically, psychologically, and socially. The dilemma of prisons as institutions purported to effect positive resocialization in a punitive, life-destroying atmosphere is not one the men inside them are unaware of:

Most prisoners are conscious of the fact that they are citizens of two worlds, within and outside walls, and the relation between the two may seem obscure and incompatible to them. They are also painfully aware of the necessity of preserving an identity relevant for life outside when release comes, while at the same time playing a role in prison however high or low its degree of relevance for life outside may be. (Galtung, in Cressey 1961, p. 113)

The barriers to meaningful rehabilitation have been noted with increasing frequency in the last decade or so, and especially since the wave of prison riots that swept the nation in the early 1970s. Nussbaum (1971) has written of enforced conformity and the suppression of any unique personal characteristics as factors mitigating against positive growth and development. Bagdikian (1972) has remarked upon the frequent isolation of state prisons in rural areas, with its concomitant destruction of valuable family ties. He alluded also to a much agreed on belief shared by most penal administrators that only 10-20 percent of all prisoners need to be locked up in the first place. But diversionary alternatives to prison are still more the exception than the rule in most communities. This is so despite an extensive analysis of 231 treatment approaches used on prisoners since 1945, which concluded that "There is very little evidence in these studies that any prevailing mode of correctional treatment has a decisive effect in reducing recidivism of convicted offenders" (p. 16).

Morris (1974) has observed that the responses to all treatment programs in which prisoners participate provide much poorer indices of postrelease criminality than do family ties, availability of a residence and job, and related extrainstitutional factors. Almost 30 years ago Shaw (1946) wrote of the debilitating and self-defeating effects of the social isolation of prison life:

When detention and restraint are necessary, the criminal's right to contact with all the spiritual influences of his day should be respected, and its exercise encouraged and facilitated. . . . This [includes] the free formation of friendship, acquaintances, marriage, in short, all the normal methods of creation and recreation, must be available for criminals as for other persons, partly because deprivation of these things is severely punitive, and partly because it is destructive to the victim, and produces what we call the criminal type, making a cure impossible. (p. 123)

In California, the names "San Quentin" and "Soledad" conjure up an immediate assortment of archetypal images of that state's solution for the convicted
felon. San Quentin began its existence a full half-century after the reformist
measures of the Quakers were initiated. Its history has been punctuated by a
long series of flamboyant administrators and wardens, and its notoriety for violence and riots continues to the present day. The much-admired Clinton Duffy,
warden during World War II, once said: "We are not running a summer resort,
but if you want men to respond like men, you've got to treat them like men."
A mere decade later his successor, Harley Teets, referred to San Quentin as a
"blindfolded elephant lumbering along the edge of a precipice" (Lamott, 1972,
p. 206). Lamott, in an interesting history of that institution, informs us that,
in 1867, the annual expenditure for each convict was $63.80, or less than 20¢
a day (p. 80)! While convicts were living under the most horrendous conditions
of inadequate food, sanitation, and medical facilities, the prison physician of
the time, one Dr. J. E. Pelham, saw fit to describe masturbation as "this dis-
gusting vice [that] undermines the constitution and debases the moral instincts
more than all other causes combined. It kills body and soul. . . " (p. 92).

Once again, it is fascinating to note that even San Quentin had its zealous
and well-intentioned beginnings. They were exemplified by the following pro-
nouncement by one of its earliest directors, Governor John Weller, in a letter
to the state assembly:

You will allow me to suggest that the practice of the courts in sending men to
prison for long periods will defeat any attempts, no matter how well directed,
at what is regarded as one of the great objects of all human punishment—
reformation. There are a number of convicts here who have, for the first offense,
been sentenced to imprisonment for ten years, and some fifteen. If a reformation cannot be effected within the first two years of confinement, there is
scarcely any hope of it. He begins to look upon the officers as his enemies,
selected by an unfeeling people to torture and oppress him. His heart becomes
callous, and all the warm and generous impulses of his soul are annihilated.
(Lamott, p. 45)

Soledad, infamous since the George Jackson trial, owes its origins to former
Governor Warren's outrage at the depravity, sadism and squalor revealed by a
special investigation he initiated of the entire state prison system. As a result,
the California Department of Corrections was organized in 1944, and the adult
authority was established to serve as a parole board (Yee, 1970, pp. 2-3). By
1946, the corrections department purchased 936 acres of land in the Salinas
Valley for a new prison described as "California's model," and in 1951, officials
opened the new institution stating that

The policy of the California State Board of Prison Directors is based upon the
concept that there can be no regeneration except in freedom. Rehabilitation,

therefore, must come from within the individual, and not through coercion. With this principle in mind, the rehabilitation program of the State Board of Prison Directors contemplates not only important educational and vocational factors, but also, by and through classification and segregation, a gradual release from custodial restraint, and corresponding increase in personal responsibility and freedom of choice. (Yee, p. 7)

Once again, lofty words yielded to developments of which the practical consequences were the converse of what had been hoped for.

California continues to be regarded nationally as being in the vanguard of progressive, rehabilitation-oriented prison systems. But the results have been anything but encouraging. Between 1959 and 1969, the median time served in that state jumped from 24 to 36 months, the longest span in the entire country. The number of persons incarcerated per 100,000 continued to rise from 65 in 1944, to 145 in 1965 (also the highest such increase in the United States). Finally, there has been no significant change in rates of recidivism (American Friends Service Committee, 1971, p. 91). The conclusion seems inescapable that after decades of trial, the treatment and rehabilitation approach has failed miserably. Not only has it not produced the desirable changes it promised, but it has led to increased numbers of human beings exposed to progressively intense suffering in the name of treatment.

Psychological Effects of Sexual Deprivation in Prison

Love is where you find it, but in prison, most times, it's in your head and hand.
— Piri Thomas (1974)

It is interesting to note that while the literature devoted to solutions of sexual deprivation in prison is negligible, descriptive writings of its devastating consequences are not so difficult to locate. This section will scan the most insightful of those commentaries as well as relevant statements made by ex-convicts whose combined time behind bars exceeds a quarter of a century.

Ibrahim (1974) remarked on the tendency of the public to ignore the critical issue of sex in prison as an even greater taboo than overt references to sexual behavior in general. He also offered several reasons for the failure of social scientists to make systematic studies in this area. These include justifiable anxiety about offending prison administrators who tend to be wary of such studies anyway, the difficulty of obtaining accurate data from inmates, and the failure of graduate departments of psychology and sociology to encourage research of this nature.

Clemmer (1958) has pointed out that "prison administrators and their associates probably have less understanding of the phenomena of sex in the closed communities they manage than any other of the perplexing problems they face each working day" (p. 378).

As early as 1948, Karpman noted that many psychoses that were the result of prison incarceration, both acute and chronic, had as their source the deprivation of normal sexual outlets, and that the disappearance of such symptoms was unexpectedly rapid as the expiration of the man's sentence approached. He lamented the institutionally induced pathology that is the cost of prison life while at the same time reflecting the social sentiment of the time when he wrote that "It is not conceivable that the prison authorities would let a prisoner's wife visit the prisoner and spend an intimate hour with him" (p. 485). Still, there was an expression of some recognition of the futility of attempting rehabilitation through punishment only, which he acknowledges leads only to hatred, humiliation, and brutalization.

Though it is difficult for an objective observer to accurately depict the deepest emotional truths of men deprived of women, some sensitive sociologists and psychologists have come close. Sykes (1958) referred to the inescapable fact that much of a man's vision of himself, his self-concept of who he is as a male, is thrown into question when he is locked up only with other men. Identity always has social determining factors, and an inmate shut off from women quickly finds that the meaning of his social existence is thrown into serious question without the emotional complementarity of the presence of women. He comes to depend for some reflective image of how he is perceived exclusively on the feedback he receives from other males, and this fractured vision is made vague and problematic by lack of contrast. The devastating effects of this isolation from a normal social milieu are rivaled only by the more personal psychological repercussions.

Lindner (1948) wrote that

No one who has not himself been a prisoner, or who has not worked with prisoners for a span of years almost to the point of merging the boundaries of his own life with theirs, can appreciate the all-pervasiveness of sex throughout the institutional atmosphere, the subtlety of its often distorted expression, and the awful impact it has upon the lives of the men, women and children confined within the walls of those social graveyards, the zoos for humans, which disgrace our landscapes and mock the pretensions of man's humanity to man. (p. 201)

Writing with the compassion of someone who had spent thousands of hours within prison walls, he writes sympathetically and with barely contained rage of the psychiatric symptoms of sexual isolation: the tendency to regressive behavior, hypnagogic states of reverie, acute panic episodes as a result of sudden homosexual feelings, uncontrollable sexual fantasies, and finally the sudden decompensation into paranoid psychosis as a last refuge from unbearable anxiety and guilt. He commented on how "the situation of heterosexual starvation. . . creates a tension-charged atmosphere that one can almost feel; and that to the fact of denial of heterosexual opportunities is due so much of the chaos, the upset, the querulousness and the electric air prison walls enclose" (p. 207).

Mention was also made of the terrible price the prisoner pays after release, in terms of unanticipated impotence problems, premature ejaculation, guilt over homosexual relations in prison, and the extraordinary difficulties of marital adjustment when the inmate is returning to a wife with whom he hasn't been intimate for several years.

Others have pointed out that the tension, irritability, and anger resulting from sexual deprivation is often augmented not only by the behavioral result- ants of involuntary masturbation, exhibitionism, and compulsive attraction to pornographic literature but also by rarely spoken of effects on the autonomic nervous system for those who refuse homosexual contact. These variously include nonspecific gastrointestinal complaints, tension headaches, and recur- rent dizzy spells (Berkey, 1971, pp. 181-83).

Kassebaum (1972) pointed out that, as far back as the seventeenth century, the keepers of Newgate Gaol in Great Britain realized that a community with- out kinship, marital bonds, or child-rearing required some form of energetic release, and hence there existed an officially unnoticed trade of prostitution within prison walls. Additionally, he referred to the deprivation of hetero- sexual contact for prisoners as "ritual deprivation" since most convicted prison- ers are drawn from the lower classes, men whose image of masculinity depends in large part on a perception of oneself as tough, virile, and attractive to women (p. 42).

Perhaps the inability to withstand the lack of sexual contact with a woman is most difficult for those men serving extremely long sentences, including life terms. Here the element of hope, and orientation toward the future, vanish to the point of desperation or resignation. Masturbation tends to become compul- sive despite reports that fantasies become increasingly difficult to conjure up on demand: "Prisoners talked of 'having been at it for hours' and relieved their concern by the usual comic references to 'going blind' and 'having it fall off' " (Cohen and Taylor, 1974, p. 83). The relationships with fellow convicts de- veloped under such circumstances must, of necessity, serve multiple functions— "One's friend. . . is not simply there for sex, or intellectual chats, or discussion of personal anxieties, or humor, or solidarity against alien forces, but for *all* these things" (p. 75). An interesting observation made along these lines is re- lated to the long-term prisoner and his almost total denial of any kind of privacy. Westin (1970) refers to four variants of privacy, namely solitude, anonymity, reserve (willful lack of self-disclosure), and intimacy. Most of us may fairly easily arrange to experience any one of these when the desire arises. However, not only are the first three of these unavailable to the prisoner because of archi- tectural, bureaucratic, and political reasons, but the last, representing the con- vergence of deep emotional and physical satisfactions, is indefinitely out of reach when a man is most in need of it.

Though there have been a spate of publications in the last decade regarding prison life written by the men who have served time, most have concerned themselves with the dehumanizing brutality of the behavior of the guards, the primitive physical conditions, and the lack of any elementary human rights. Still, a few convicts from time to time have focused on the sexual tensions and dilemma inherent in "doing time." More than 40 years ago, Victor Nelson quoted Oscar Wilde's "Ballad of Reading Gaol":

> And the fetid breath of living death
> Chokes up each grated screen;
> And all, but Lust, is turned dust
> In Humanity's Machine.

He then wrote from his own experience, asserting that

. . . of all the possible forms of starvation, surely none is more demoralizing than sexual starvation. . . . To the man dying of hunger and thirst it makes very little difference that the only available food and water are tainted. Likewise it makes very little or no difference to the average prisoner that the only available means of sexual satisfaction are abnormal. It is merely a matter of satisfying as best he can the hunger which besets him. I mean a hunger not only for sexual intercourse, but a hunger for the voice, the touch, the laugh, the tears of Woman, a hunger for Woman Herself. (Nelson, 1932, p. 143)

Piri Thomas, a Puerto Rican ex-convict, compared the yearning for a woman as the months pass into years as rivaled only by the desire for freedom itself. He argued that if conjugal visits or weekend passes are proscribed, then prisons should at least be coed.

By being able to treat each other as peers, man to woman, and fall in love with each other, we would retrieve our identity as human beings. It would ease the pain of loneliness and fulfill the human right to feel love and express emotions. . . all the substitutes for heterosexual relationships in prison do not make the inmates perverted. It is the society that is perverted by perpetuating this negation of normal expressions of love. (Thomas, 1974, pp. 140-41)

One of the most interesting accounts of the torment of sexual deprivation comes from Morton Sobell, who served almost 20 years in federal prisons after being convicted of espionage with Julius and Ethel Rosenberg. While still awaiting trial, he described how he and his wife constructed individual sexual fantasies that they conveyed to each other in code language through letters and during visits. After conviction and while still in New York during the period of legal appeals, he related a subsequent stage of his need to adjust to new sexual realities: "I hadn't planned it, it came out spontaneously. Suddenly I asked, 'Helen, have you been sleeping with anyone?' Without a moment's hesitation she responded, 'I have.' The shock was unlike anything I had ever before experienced. . . . In one single moment my sense of security was totally destroyed. For me her action represented hopelessness" (Sobell, 1974, p. 315). Later, on reflecting on what had occurred, he commented, "Actually, it was not primarily the idea of Helen's having sexual intercourse with another man that disturbed me, so much as *the danger I felt it posed to our future relationship.* This might be the first step away from *me*" (pp. 319-20, emphasis added). In all these first person accounts of men deprived of sexual intimacy with women it is significant that emotional losses are stressed at least as much, if not more than, the absence of physical gratification per se.

Homosexuality in Prison

I have been in prisons in three states and have seen homosexuality destroy men who thought they would never have anything to do with such behavior.
                                                                      —Torok, 1973

No one mindful of the extraordinary intensity of sexual hunger after prolonged deprivation is surprised that homosexuality in prison, as in any single-sex institution, is inevitable. For obvious reasons, statistics reflecting the incidence of homosexual activity in prison are hard to come by, although estimates made by careful researchers vary from 14 percent (Roth, 1971) to 32 percent (Clemmer, 1958). Taking into account the understandable reluctance to acknowledge participation in what is still regarded as deviant behavior, the figure may well be double the larger of these approximations, especially in facilities that have a younger population.

The motivation for such behavior is not the simple longing for sexual release. Rather, there are multiple determinants that take into account more global needs and tensions. These include "some social or psychological need such as loneliness or passivity, the desire to be taken care of, the desire to dominate someone, an erotic substitution for depression, chaotic emotional states involving fear and rage, and re-enactment of some earlier sexual or non-sexual experience" (Allen, 1969, p. 297). Closely allied to these factors are the search for a meaningful emotional relationship of some durability as a substitute for the impossible man-woman union as well as an attempt to confirm one's masculinity by resisting the environment through controlling a sexual partner.

Clearly many men in prison have had homosexual orientations since puberty. Such men, in prisons which tolerate noncoercive homosexual contact, need not suffer the anguish of the heterosexual prisoner, stimulated on the one hand by the intense longing for sexual intimacy and wracked on the other by overwhelming feelings of homosexual guilt. The persons who suffer most under these circumstances are those young men still in late adolescence or their early twenties, whose sexual identity may be permanently warped after their first experience with sodomy or fellatio. And for those men who will be returning to wives, the problems are complicated geometrically. Kinsey (1948) has spoken of the often irreparable damage to young husbands under these conditions. No wonder then that in circumstances of this sort "visits can be torture for a man separated from his wife by heavy screen wire, a glass window or a table" (Martin, 1951, p. 182).

The attitude of the prison administrators to homosexuality, while the very epitome of hypocrisy, tends to serve institutional needs. While it may be condoned when it takes place among the "right" people (cooperative men who have become submissive zombies), its occurrence among the "wrong" inmates is severely punished, either by being thrown into solitary or, worse yet, by having a letter sent to a man's family and loved ones describing various perverse acts he has engaged in (Torok, 1973). Where it is tolerated it may be used to blackmail men, or to permit the release of tensions that might otherwise lead to violence, while simultaneously avoiding any possibility of the public learning of its existence. Penal authorities know that citizens would rather not know what goes on in the prisons that their tax money supports. The more brutal and simpleminded of the guards use it as a source of confirming their own moral superiority: "It's in them. I couldn't believe it could happen till I saw it, and I had to give them both the hole. . . . There must be something wrong with every man here else he wouldn't be here" (Weinberg, 1942, p. 721).

The simple fact is that prisons make no real allowance for the natural tension that results from idleness, monotony, and boredom, all exacerbated by the uncontrollable accumulation of sexual energy. The inevitable result is homosexual assault and rape on a scale that has only recently begun to be documented. Thomas (1974) wrote that "Intimidated by threats of death and mutilation, these youngsters lacked the strength and courage to resist and thus became human receptacles for other inmates' sexual release. . . . No wonder the highest rate of mental illness was among these youngsters, not to mention suicide attempts, successful and unsuccessful (p. 138)."

Weiss and Friar, in their book *Terror in the Prisons: Homosexual Rape and Why Society Condones It* (1974), catalog a series of brutal sexual assaults so sustained and so unchecked that one can only conclude that there are virtually no administrative controls over sadistic acts so long as they occur *between convicts*. It is sadly ironic that the forms of sexual behavior that are fostered in prison are condemned by a majority of the population when they occur in society at large. And the varieties of psychopathic sexual aggression seem to have no bounds. In one account, a prisoner seized by the descriptions in the pornographic *Story of O* compelled a convicted investment banker to wear a wooden cylinder in his anus for several weeks as well as raping him almost daily (Haggerty, 1975, p. 42).

Only in the last ten years or so have allegations of homosexual assault been the object of any official inquiry. Perhaps the most extensive and publicized investigation thus far has been the one carried out jointly by the Philadelphia District Attorney's office and the Police Department of that city in 1968. It

was initiated by a court-ordered demand after repeated incidents of brutal homosexual rapes. The report is noteworthy because of its scope and detail: 3,304
inmates and 561 prison staff people interviewed, 130 written statements taken,
and 45 polygraph examinations administered, all over a two year period. A five
percent sample of prisoners revealed 156 assaults and 97 victims. Bearing in
mind the considerable and understandable resistance of inmates to disclose
their victimization in such assaults, it was extrapolated that during the period
investigated there were 2,000 assaults, involving 1,500 victims and 3,500 aggres-
sors (Davis, 1968, pp. 2-3).

The report further found that the frustrations causing such attacks were as
much sociological and cultural as they were psychological in nature. They were
derived from the same inability while outside prison to achieve a sense of mas-
culine identification and pride through extrasexual routes such as careers,
families, and social activities. The attacks then were seen as the consequence of
the intensification of these frustrations combined with racial hostility and the
primitive notion of sex as an act of aggression and subjugation (p. 4).

In discussing the "abnormal" conditions of prison life responsible for
homosexual rape, the investigators commented that "heterosexual relationships,
even the most moral and lawful are strictly forbidden. . . . The double wire
screens have been removed from the visiting room for certain prisoners who can
be trusted to 'touch the forbidden fruit lightly but not eat thereof. . .' " (p. 71,
emphasis added). Finally, in their recommendations for effecting drastically
needed change, they suggest that if prisoners

were permitted conjugal visits, many family relationships might be saved, tensions relieved and a higher morality introduced into the prison social structure.
Such a program would require the construction of security cottages where man
and wife could spend time privately together. It has been accomplished in as
primitive a state as Mississippi; it can and should be done in Philadelphia. (p. 66)

Sexual Deprivation and the Prisoner's Family

For married prisoners the beginning of a prison term often means the end of all
those things they need, value, and cherish about family life. And surely the loss
of a man's freedom cannot help but rupture the regular pattern of interactions
with his wife and children. What is not clear is just how total and unyielding to
qualification society intends for this separation to be. The literature relating
imprisonment to marital and family relationships is almost nonexistent. To
some extent this probably reflects a generalized feeling that men in prison *ipso
facto* forfeit the right to continue any semblance of family life, and deservedly
so. Outside of regular visiting programs, there exists only one institutional
attempt in this country to actively engage a wife and family in programs that

can affect the husband's future. Sponsored by the Rosenberg Foundation in 1959, it made available funds to the California Department of Corrections to provide for a family counseling project that included films, lectures, discussions, group and couples therapy, and systematic prerelease meetings that included prison personnel, the parolee, and his wife and children. The program was discontinued when grant funds expired (Fenton, 1959).

Indeed some men sentenced for several years prefer not to see their family at all given the emotional strain of maintaining a relationship under the most frustrating and painful of circumstances. As one expressed it, "I don't do hard time. It's much easier if you get the outside off your mind and just forget about your family, your folks and your wife" (Farber in Lewin, 1944, p. 176). A three year study of 800 prisoners revealed that practically no official interest exists in mobilizing the family for purposes of postparole adjustment to society. The resultant loneliness and sexual frustration of most of these men as their families began to slip more and more into the background resulted in an onslaught of physical symptoms manifested most frequently by acute anxiety, insomnia, fainting, and general fatigue (Morris, 1965, p. 296).

Clemmer (1965) regards the maintenance of family and love objects in the community as one of the most salient factors in restricting men from engaging in sexual activities of a sort that they would not ordinarily endorse. Additionally he points out that many wives of prisoners divorce and remarry:

Such a step on a woman's part means a broken home for the prisoner, who, when he does re-enter the outside world goes out with much bitterness in his heart. . . . The one thing that may have worked out as his salvation, his reformation, that is, preserved family ties, is lacking, and if he fails to make good who can say how much of this failure can be laid at the door of his broken home. (p. 258)

Howlett (1973) has discovered that the first victims of marital dissolution in prison are those newlyweds whose foundations were just barely established prior to confinement. He has noted that the first two years are critical for determining whether or not the wife will continue to maintain the relationship, and that one may almost directly observe the vicissitudes of the marriage in the man's discipline problems or their absence within the institution. Those family relationships that have existed for longer periods weather the storm of imprisonment longer, although the attendant emotional suffering is proportionately greater. He observes that perhaps the only hope for the preservation of the family are accommodations with adequate custodial safeguards where prisoners and spouses can enjoy conjugal visits (p. 8).

A recent study (Williams and Elder, 1970) found that the wives of men in prison are subjected to a barrage of psychological problems, including social ostracism, guilt, loneliness, anxiety, and depression. But, they concluded that "By far the greatest effect of separation of the wives was the psycho-sexual effects. The husband-wife relationship was shattered. . . the universal expression by 15 [wives] was that the companionship dreamt about, thought of, and worked at for some time was gone, and with it great emotional needs and inter-dependence" (p. 210). Of 17 wives studied, three secured divorces, two involved themselves in common-law relationships, and two admitted to having affairs. It is clear that when a married man is incarcerated an entire social system is upset. The conclusions drawn on the basis of this study were succinctly expressed:

The evidence would tend to show that the complete isolation of the husband from the wife for a number of years had deleterious effects on the family and places it under such strain that its survival or rebuilding potentialities were ex-ceedingly small. Some new approach must of necessity be found if society and the community in general are not to become the victims of their own vigilance. (P. 212)

Legal Aspects of Sex Deprivation in Prison

. . . when we cease to consider what the criminal deserves and consider only what will cure him or deter others, we have tacitly removed him from the sphere of justice altogether; instead of a person, a subject of rights, we now have a mere object, a patient, a "case."

— C. S. Lewis (in Killinger and Cromwell, 1973)

The social cataclysms of the 1960s, the surge of prison riots that began around 1970, and the growth of a sustained prisoners' rights movement have all combined to make the issue of sexual deprivation in prison more and more the subject of judicial opinion. And the pivotal mainspring of those who contend that its legit-imacy is unworthy of further sanction is that "The convict is sent to prison to be deprived of his liberty and compelled to labor as an expiation of his crime, and any other punishment besides that which is absolutely necessary to accomplish this and enforce the discipline of the prison is not only unlawful but inhuman. (Lamott, 1972, p. 47)

As far back as 1944, in the federal case of *Coffin* v. *Reich*, the court stated that "a prisoner retains all rights of an ordinary citizen except those expressly, or by necessary implication, taken from him by law" (National Council on Crime and Delinquency, 1972, p. 44). Of course, it has been left to administrative fiat to determine precisely with what latitude this noble statement may be interpreted.

Of those responsible for the nuts and bolts custodial jobs at most state prisons, there are a considerable number who believe in the "they ain't got nothin' coming to them" philosophy. They are vigorously opposed to the senti-ments of groups like the American Friends Service Committee which has pro-posed a prisoners' bill of rights advocating that prisoners are entitled to all constitutional rights guaranteed to free persons except when those would be inconsistent with the operation of the institution. It is implicit in this concept that the burden of explanation ought to be on the facility to show good cause for the deprivation of consensual sexual relations, rather than on the prisoner to demonstrate its legitimacy.

The district attorney's office in Philadelphia probably set a precedent when, in its report on sexual assaults in prisons, they drew the following conclusion: "It is a system which imposes a cruel, gruesome punishment which is not, and could not, be included in the sentence of the court. . . . Since it is a system which exists under the aegis of the court and the community, it is the duty of the court and the community to destroy it" (Davis, 1968, p. 17). More specifically, in addressing themselves to homosexual rape, they regard the court as inherently responsible for the situation and consequently obliged to expose such situations and eliminate them whenever they are discovered.

One may wonder why the courts have needed until now to assume the social responsibilities which their legal powers imply. One reason is historically reflected in the *Banning* v. *Looney* (1954) decision which initiated the "hands-off doctrine" stating that courts were "without power to supervise prison administrators or to interfere with the ordinary prison rules or regulations" (Murphy, 1973, p. 442).

This perspective left convicts without enforceable rights so long as the institution could provide a rationale to demonstrate that any measure it took was in the service of efficient administrative operation. But then, in 1962, in a landmark decision (*Winston* v. *United States*) the U.S. Federal District Court rejected this doctrine, claiming that some deprivations could clearly be seen to be the work of capricious and arbitrary decisions and as such could not be judicially endorsed. Reference was made to the *Coffin* decision, cited above. Since legal precedents are not invariably succeeded by social fact, penal administrators have not been much intimidated nor compelled to alter their traditional policies. But many recognize that the absolute tyranny over men's lives that has customarily been available to those administrators is now being seriously questioned in many quarters.

More and more prisoners are filing suit as a means of testing to what extent the lack of conjugal visits may be unconstitutional. The thrust of their argument has been: (1) either that the absence of such visits fosters a homosexual orientation in men who are heterosexual; or, (2) that it often exposes the less formidably built of the prisoners to brutal and continuous sexual assaults. In either case, the claim is made that the result violates the Eighth Amendment safeguard against "cruel and unusual punishment." In a recent decision (*Stuart* v. *Heard*, 359 Fed. Supp. 1973), a class action was brought by a group of prisoners claiming a constitutional right to be housed in coed prisons and to have regularly scheduled conjugal visits with their spouses. The court, while it supported the view that such changes had obvious social value, denied the plaintiffs' request, expressing the belief that policy decisions of the sort that had been sued for are properly and exclusively a legislative matter (pp. 922-23).

Three years earlier, in *Holt* v. *Sarver*, inmates in the Arkansas prison system brought an action against correctional authorities based on the unconstitutionality of conditions prevailing in that prison system. One of the conditions specified was the widespread fear of homosexual rape, and fights and stabbings associated with such assaults. It is important to note that *Stuart* v. *Heard* was a case decided in Texas while the present case was brought in Arkansas. Since the administration of prisons (except for federal crimes) is a function reserved to the states, no judicial decision in this arena will be binding across states, nor does a court's ruling insure that change will inevitably follow.

In any event, the court stated in the *Holt* case that

The concept of "cruel and unusual punishment" is not limited to instances in which a particular inmate is subjected to a punishment directed at him as an individual. In the Court's estimation confinement itself within a given institution may amount to a cruel and unusual punishment prohibited by the Constitution where the confinement is characterized by conditions and practices so bad as to be shocking to the conscience of reasonably civilized people. (Danziger, 1971, pp. 430-31)

In the same year, in Louisiana, this identical principle was the basis of yet another case, *Hamilton* v. *Schiro*, in which once again inmates contended that continued exposure to sexual assaults violated the Eighth Amendment. The court found for the plaintiffs and stated that confinement in such a setting "shocks the conscience as a matter of elemental decency" (Danziger, p. 431). Decisions of this sort have provoked legal scholars to begin to articulate the obvious deduction that "Conjugal visiting has been suggested as a program which could possibly decrease the dangers of sexual attack. . . . It is believed that allowing husbands and wives to have sexual relations in prison or as an alternative, allowing home visits may stabilize a prisoner's marital relationship and aid in his rehabilitation. (Danziger, p. 437)

Conjugal Visits in Foreign Penitentiaries

The existence of conjugal visiting programs in the penitentiaries of many countries outside the United States is generally attributable to two basic factors: a less puritancial and hypocritical attitude about sex, and/or a greater emphasis on the cultural value of the family as a primary and vital social unit. Conrad (1970) and Ward (1972) have written with admiration of such visits in Swedish and Danish prisons where the men get weekly visits by their wives in their own rooms for periods of three to nine hours. Such visits, together with home furloughs, are regarded not as privileges but *"as a matter of right"* (Conrad, p. 135, emphasis added).

Even in isolated Russian prison colonies,

the sexual drives of the colonists are realistically respected. Abstinence is neither required nor encouraged. An occasional interlude with a wife in a dismal guest house scarcely meets the conditions of romance or even of dignity, but as a maintenance of marital realities and as relief of infectious sexual tension it makes more sense than the cat-and-mouse homosexuality so common in Western prisons. (Conrad, p. 165)

The government considers the program significant enough to pay the wives' travel expenses to and from the camps.

Cavan and Zemans (1958) found that not only did several nations in Europe, Latin America, and the Far East permit conjugal visits, but that some such as India, Pakistan, the Philippines, and Mexico all have specific penal colonies where prisoners can live with their families for the duration of their sentences. After admitting that "The general impression received . . . is that many countries hold a more humanitarian attitude toward prisoners than do many groups in the U.S.," they rather strangely conclude that "conjugal visits in prison are not compatible with mores in the United States, since they seem to emphasize only the physical satisfactions of sex" (p. 139).

The most recent survey of international penal practices regarding conjugal visits reveals that they are solidly established and sanctioned by official policy in each of the following countries: Bolivia, Brazil, Burma, Canada, Chile, Columbia, Costa Rica, Denmark, Equador, El Salvador, Guatemala, Honduras, India, Japan, Mexico, Pakistan, Peru, the Philippines, Poland, Puerto Rico, the Soviet Union, Sweden, and Venezuela (Hopper, 1969, p. 6).

In Mexico, where the cult of machismo extends even behind prison walls, conjugal visits are believed to prevent homosexuality and to preserve the all-important family ties that are inextricably bound to religious (Catholic) considerations. Again, it is viewed as an essential "right," not as a special reward, so that in 1947, when they were abolished in the federal penitentiary in Mexico City, the result was widespread rioting that resulted in their restoration within a week (Hopper, p. 7).

In India, at the prison colony in Bombay, men may live with their wives in separate cottages and wear civilian clothes. Almost all have jobs within the facility that enable them to sustain their families during the period of incarceration. A similar structure exists at Mexico's Tres Marias Penal Colony, located 90 miles off the Pacific coast: ". . . here a prisoner can live with his wife and children very much like he would in any other community. He does not wear a prison uniform except one day a month when he has to appear before a counseling board. Both male and female single inmates are allowed to marry and bring their spouses to the colony" (Hopper, p. 9). Finally, Columbia is tolerant enough to allow inmates to visit licensed houses of prostitution bi-weekly for periods of up to two hours.

Attitudes Toward Conjugal Visits in the United States

And the two shall become one flesh, so that there are no longer two, but one flesh. What therefore God has united—let not man separate or divide.
                                                                        —Mark 10:8-9

Throughout the historical expansion of the state prison systems in this country, two distinct themes have been sounded on the issue of the appropriateness or social usefulness of conjugal visits. One has been avowedly conservative and oppositional. The other, mindful of practices in other countries and of the ugly tensions stirred by sexual deprivation in prison, has tried to educate a public increasingly victimized by criminals to the potential advantages of initiating or even contemplating such visits as a matter of official policy. It is, of course, no accident that the former sentiments have been articulated mainly by the correctional establishment and right-wing politicans, while the latter has been put forth by liberal sociologists and psychologists, muckracking journalists, and ex-convicts. Despite their controversial nature, the arguments espoused by both sides 30 years ago remain essentially unchanged today.

It is especially interesting to examine the writings of those well-intentioned social scientists who acknowledge the social and psychological benefits of conjugal visits in one breath only to avoid advocating their establishment in the next on the basis of the most shallow of moral grounds. Most characteristic in this respect are Zemans and Cavan (1958) and Barnes and Teeters (1959). It should be borne in mind that both pairs of authors are regarded as exemplars of an enlightened liberal-reformist philosophy. The first pair of authors, after doing a fairly extensive study of marital relationships of prisoners, made several significant discoveries. They found that the rate of divorce among men in prisons is four to seven times that of the general population. They further noted that when released the ex-convict needs a solid support system to assist him in getting back on his feet, and that the family is in an ideal position to assume this role. They observed finally that marriages are worth preserving despite the incarceration of the husband because most men do not serve long terms. Surprisingly they found that the median time served in federal prisons was 11 months, with 96 percent of prisoners released by the fifth year of imprisonment. The comparable figures for state prisons were a 21 month median term, with 90 percent released by the fifth year (Zemans and Cavan, p. 53).

One might think that the facts enumerated above would naturally have led to the advancement of conjugal visits at the earliest possible time. On the contrary, Zemans and Cavan added their own support to the status quo, refusing to recommend conjugal visits because they had little or no approval among prison administrators, and because they believed such visits to offer only limited physical satisfactions (p. 57)! Their recommendation was a program of home furloughs for carefully selected men, toward the end of their sentence.

Barnes and Teeters also maintained a preference for home furloughs, and were even more confounding in their attitude toward conjugal visits. They were quite direct in lauding other countries that have such visits as reflecting a humane and progressive perspective, even going so far as describing visits to prostitutes in Latin America without being pejorative. But the following comments are most revealing of the timidity that intellectuals have been so often accused:

Periodically one reads of sexual or conjugal visiting in some of the Latin countries. This *sensible* practice is consistent with the mores of several countries, *but it would be inappropriate in our Anglo-Saxon culture.* . . .
There are many practices in the correctional field that seem to work well in other countries yet would not be popular or even acceptable, in the United States. It is quite doubtful if members of the families of prisoners would wish to "move in" to a prison compound, even if houses were provided. (Barnes and Teeters, p. 510-11, emphasis added)

This latter statement was not demonstrably true at the time, nor, as this study will show, is it true now.

In the midsixties two studies appeared that focused specifically on the views of penal administrators on conjugal visits. Balough (1964) sent questionnaires to 52 wardens. While the majority were unequivocally opposed to them, 13 percent surprisingly indicated an affirmative stance (p. 56). A year later in a similar survey Vedder (1965) received responses from 49 directors of state and federal facilities. While a comparable majority figure were still against such visits, the proportion that favored them was twice as large as in the Balough study (p. 52). The reasons offered for the rejection of such a program ran a considerable gamut, including concern over unwanted pregnancies, discrimination against single inmates, overemphasis on the value of sex in marriage, financial limitations, unfavorable public opinion, the insult to the dignity of wives, and security and custodial problems. The reasons for being opposed to conjugal visits offered by respondents were uniformly remarkable in that they concerned themselves with the needs and opinions of society, the prison staff, unborn babies, and the state budget—thereby ignoring only the needs of the prisoners.

As late as 1971, Johns, in an article aptly titled "Alternatives to Conjugal Visiting," reiterates the aforementioned factors as justification for no conjugal visits. He too suggested, however, a furlough system instead, despite his apprehensions about the possible escapes, legal offenses, and unwanted pregnancies that might eventuate from them. A 1972 inquiry addressed to all 50 state correctional departments revealed that only two states presently had provisions for conjugal visiting: Mississippi and California. The thrust of the article was summed up in the comment, "Furloughs accomplish the goals of conjugal visits, and in addition are much more normal and eliminate the possibility of degradation" (Markley, 1972, p. 22). What the advocates of furloughs have failed to consider

is how tiny a proportion of prisoners such programs serve, and that they are
generally available only to men who are within a few months of their final
release date.

Concurrent with the appearance of the literature cited above there has
appeared a less professionally publicized and occasionally more polemically expressed viewpoint typified by remarks such as Martin's some 20 years ago:
"Conjugal visits . . . if proposed openly, undoubtedly would meet with the utmost
resistance from everybody except the inmates and their wives and sweethearts.
Nevertheless, righteous citizens who oppose them ought to ponder the alternative,
which is the present abomination" (Martin, 1954, p. 182). These were heretical
words in the midfifties, as were the author's comments on the not so subtle
political aspects of such visits. He commented that "conjugal visits could be
allowed as routine, or allowed a few as a reward for good behavior, depending
upon whether we believe that to deprive prisoners of sexual outlets is to create
an administrative problem or that to do so is to deprive them of their rights as
men" (p. 182).

One of the earliests records of concern expressed for the sex life of men in
prison can be attributed to Fishman (1934), who very much admired the enlightened attitude shown by many foreign countries in this regard. He considered those nations as more realistic while simultaneously lamenting the negative
cast of public opinion in the U.S. regarding this issue. Reluctantly, then, he
proposed, at that early date, a simple furlough system for married and unmarried
inmates alike. This alternative, he hoped, would be found more palatable by the
American public. His book grew out of a federal study on prison conditions
and in his final recommendations he suggested that scheduled visits home to
one's wife or girlfriend would serve several worthwhile goals. It would tend to
keep the family together, diminish homosexual activity, and prevent personality
defects that might arise from sustained sexual suppression (p. 184).

He quotes Ramon Lopez Jiminez, cabinet officer and prison reformer in
Ecuador, as an indication of just how reactionary U.S. penal policies were at the
time. Jiminez said,

The spiritual torture of those who lose their liberty is still more severe if one
remembers that those unfortunate individuals have left behind in their homes
their life companions, the wives to whom they made vows of love before Church
and state. It is quite *legal* to deny the prisoners life, often to deny them air, to
deny them liberty, to forget them in their prisons, but the law does not deny
them their rights as men. (Fishman, p. 179)

In concluding his study, Fishman made the first statement in this country
on behalf of initiating a program of conjugal visits in penal institutions. But he
was sophisticated enough to know that "Whether or not a system of this nature
will some day be inaugurated in our prisons will, in the last analysis, rest with
that invisible but potent force—public opinion. In the light of all the facts

presented, we believe it merits serious consideration, and an attempt to put it on a working basis" (p. 188).

Only in the last five years or so has there been the beginning of a consistent set of voices challenging the prevailing conservatism on the issue of sexual deprivation of prisoners, and especially those with wives. Haynor (1972) reviewed the policies of other countries and suggested that American policymakers might need to reconsider their archaic position. Braswell and DeFrancis (1972) pointed out that the psychological stresses caused by having no appropriate sexual outlet severely constrain any rehabilitative efforts. They expressed concern too that in an environment where men have no intimate, tender contact with women their essential feeling of "maleness" is thrown into question. The result often leads to acute anxiety and doubt concerning their self-image as men. The authors indicated a preference for home furloughs to alleviate sexual tensions, but also recommended conjugal visiting rights as having additional value. Thus, an interesting transitional point of view is represented here, with some of the old reservations raised, but allied now to a willingness to at least explore such visits as a feasible alternative to the present situation.

One of the most concise and cogent statements of advocacy for the psychosocial value of allowing wives to have sexual visits with their husbands in prison comes from a man who works within the system—Dr. Robert Sheldon, chief of psychiatry for the Texas Department of Corrections. He wrote,

Conjugal visitation could be instituted in many prison settings without disruption of proper procedures and with a lessening of tension and frustration. Complete isolation of men and women from all sexual activities of a heterosexual nature is completely unrealistic and results in homosexual behavior or in other displacement of the sexual drive in hostile, aggressive and sometimes dangerous behavior toward other inmates and prison personnel. Maintenance of some family communication and integrity by the inmate's being with his wife and children would certainly lessen the high number of divorces which occur after a man goes to prison and provide for a more stable living situation to return to after his prison term has ended. (Sheldon, 1972, pp. 20-21)

A mixture of good intentions and narrow vision was reflected in Rieger's proposal for combining conjugal visits with family therapy (1973). The author worked at a federal penitentiary for two years doing mainly psychiatric crisis intervention. He observed that the most common precipitation of emotional stress was connected to the termination of a relationship with a wife or girlfriend. Of 58 suicide attempts, more were caused by the loss of a loved one than by any other factor. Of the men whose wives left them because of their imprisonment he noted an increased injury to already low self-esteem with the likelihood of recidivism increased accordingly. He stated, "I was impressed with the enormous human suffering caused by the separation of couples who had lived in a marriage or arrangement of average compatibility" (p. 118).

Despite the generally positive nature of his suggestions, Rieger qualified any endorsement of a universal visiting program that would allow married prisoners intimate contact with their wives by advancing a set of eligibility criteria including an assessment of the inmate's motivation, length of sentence, and evaluation of the prisoner's wife. It is this kind of moralizing which informs the notion of *privileged* opportunities, as contrasted with the belief that even for prisoners there exist certain inalienable *rights.*

Haggerty (1975), after offering a series of vignettes of brutal homosexual rapes in prison, advocated conjugal visits as "the most imaginative solution devised thus far" (p. 123). Perhaps Chaneles (1973), a sociologist with substantial experience in corrections work, was most radical of all, contending that conjugal visits should not be limited to wives, but should also include

sweethearts, common-law parties and intimate friends. . . . [Also] for those whose mode of sexual behavior is homosexual, homosexual relations should be permitted among consenting prisoners as well as with homosexual partners from outside of prison. For those whose only means for finding sexual expression is through the payment of prostitutes, male or female, prostitutes should be allowed to practice their occupation [in prison]. (p. 123)

It does not appear probable that such statements will be considered with anything but mockery and derision for some time in the future. Nevertheless, such recommendations have been useful in making less revolutionary proposals more acceptable.

It has been amply documented that the spectrum of attitudes regarding conjugal visits in this nation's prisons has been at best unenthusiastic, and at worst flagrantly hostile. Yet despite the massive and consistent sentiment against such programs, there has existed one beacon of sanity from the most unexpected of quarters. It first came to public attention when a one column article appeared in the New York *Times* in August 1967, buried on page 26. It announced "Conjugal Visits in Prison Hailed" and the lead paragraph read, "Conjugal visits for married inmates in Mississippi State Penetentiary have probably kept marriages intact and have probably bolstered morale, and reduced recidivism and homo-sexuality" (New York *Times*, August 15, 1967).

The fact is, incongruous as it seems, that up until 1968, Mississippi was the only state in the country that had an ongoing and extremely successful conjugal visiting program at its state prison in Parchman. Up until 1966, wives visited every Sunday for two hours. Since then the plan has been modified to every other Sunday for a four hour period. "One man, who had been employed there intermittently for over 35 years and who lived near the penitentiary and had knowledge of it even before his employment, said that conjugal visits were allowed as long ago as 1918" (Hopper, 1969a, p. 52).

On visiting days each man whose wife has showed up is given a key to one of the eight by ten foot "red houses" set up for that purpose. The rooms are scattered in six different areas throughout the 21,000 acres of this rural prison. They are furnished with beds, tables, and mirrors, and while simple in design they seem suitable to the inmates and their wives. Children also visit, and are often minded by camp personnel so that a man and his wife may have some private time alone. Single prisoners who were interviewed have not indicated any resentment about ineligibility to participate themselves. One, in fact, highly endorsed the program and said that because of the visits "I have seen less rioting, less homosexuality, and an altogether different attitude in the inmates in general" (*Times*, p. 26).

It is important to note that no restrictions are imposed on those who may participate, based either on the nature of the crime committed or for any disciplinary problems within the camp itself. Such a policy clearly reflects the administration's strong emphasis on family contacts, as well as its belief that the visits are a right that cannot and will not be denied on the basis of other factors that do not speak well for the inmate. This philosophy was echoed by a camp sergeant who said:

I don't know of anything that's more important. It's a touching sight to see a man and his wife greet each other on visiting day. I'd hate to have to tell my men that conjugal visiting was going to stop. Not only because of the fuss it might cause, but because *I believe it's the right thing to do.* You just look at the faces of these men on visiting day and you can see it. (Hopper, 1969a, p. 259, emphasis added)

It will be important to bear this perspective in mind when the family visiting program at Soledad is described in a later chapter.

Hopper, who has done the most extensive study of the Mississippi program, has repeatedly emphasized the necessity of viewing a prisoner's sexual needs as ultimately more emotional than purely biological (1969a, 1971). He has written "What a person really wants from a sexual experience is an intimate interpersonal relationship. He wants to prove that he is desirable and that he is able to evoke a response from another person. In short, he wants to demonstrate that he is adequate as a person" (1971, p. 75). He expressed doubt that prisons will ever effectively rehabilitate men unless provisions are made for their sexual needs.

He may, however, have been somewhat pollyannish, or perhaps may be simply reflecting a Southern sensibility when he says, "If a man's family includes his wife, then we must let him retain his marital rights with her. The public will accept and even applaud programs which are built around the family. All people know the importance of the family" (1971, p. 76). He was vigorous in his conviction that at least as important as the sexual gratification itself is a man's ability to maintain an image of himself as someone important to others, a need totally eradicated in the prison environment. He referred as well to the general good will generated by a prisoner's experiencing a measure of dignity conferred by penal authorities who have demonstrated that inmates are regarded as men, and "men who have basic human rights" (1971, p. 76).

Conjugal Visits in California

California has long had a reputation as one of the most progressive states in the country in its treatment of criminals and in its prison policies in general. It is a reputation little earned and less warranted, though this is not the place to detail why that is so. However, at the present time it *does* have the distinction of being the only state besides Mississippi that permits conjugal visits to its married prisoners.

The seeds of the present policy may well have begun back in 1952 when the warden at the California Institution for Men made what was then a radical change in visiting conditions for prisoners at that facility. Whereas formerly visits were of a noncontact nature for one hour, now they were to take place in an outdoor setting every Sunday from 11:00 AM until 3:00 PM. A prisoner was allowed to touch and embrace his wife within acceptable limits of propriety, and to share a relaxed lunch with his family at tree-lined picnic tables. The following remarks by an inmate and his wife indicate just how valuable this seemingly minor change actually was for them:

Prisoner: My wife hasn't missed a Sunday in 19 months and I really believe that has kept us together . . . you feel like a man again.
Wife: It used to take me 14 hours to travel 500 miles north to see him for just one short hour, then 14 hours back again. You can't think of anything to say in one hour. I was half scared and we just sat and looked at each other across a counter. (Scudder, 1952, p. 159)

In 1968, the state prison at Tehachapi initiated conjugal visits on a pilot basis, the intention being to extend the program throughout the state if it was deemed successful there. It was, and is currently, referred to as the "family visiting program" because in addition to wives, men may also be visited for this extended period by their parents, siblings, and children. Still, as will be seen later, most of the family visits that actually take place include a man's wife. The stated purpose of the department of corrections in starting the program was to foster family stability and to facilitate postrelease adjustment as a productive citizen. It was believed that these two goals interlocked in that strengthened family ties would maximize a successful reentry into the community.

The criteria for participation were six months of good conduct, "minimum custody" status, and no past involvement in smuggling of contraband. The visits were 46 hours long and took place in two apartments on prison grounds. A large fenced in playground for children was immediately adjacent to the housing facilities. The family was expected to provide food for the entire duration of the visit. This was welcomed by most prisoners as an opportunity to eat something other than the standard prison fare for two days (Lloyd, 1969). A prisoner who took part in the program at that time made the following interesting comments:

It was a return to reality, a shedding of the "skin" of prison-oriented thinking, if only briefly. Now I know that this skin is not irremovable . . . If a marriage is supposed to survive a penal separation, this program will help preserve it. If not, it will avoid an explosive parole situation . . . I can think of no other program sponsored by the Department of Corrections that has meant so much to me. (p. 146)

A few years later, when the program had clearly begun to establish its value, Lawrence Wilson, the deputy director of the corrections department, was interviewed as part of a broad survey of the feelings of penal administrators toward conjugal visits. Mr. Wilson was direct and straightforward in asserting that society does not gain protection by the dissolution of the family units of which prisoners are a part. Focusing on its social justification he said: "The fact that husbands and wives engage in sexual intercourse is incidental to our main objectives: the preservation and strengthening of the family" (Haynor, 1972, p. 49). He indicated there was little public opposition once people were able to relate to the goal of family preservation. He claimed, too, that many wives had abandoned separation plans after regular participation in the family visits.

Despite the uniqueness of California's family visiting program and its singular popularity with inmates, almost no research on it has appeared since its inception. The single exception is a study conducted five years ago at the Southern Conservation Center in Chino involving 843 inmates (Holt and Miller, 1972). Their preface stated that "Although [visiting] arrangements have existed since the beginning of prisons in this state, little systematic information is available about the nature and consequences of these outside contacts" (p. vi). They further observed that "While there is little information about the impact of prison on recidivism, personalities, or values, there is even less about its effects on family relationships. A reasonably thorough search of the literature failed to turn up even one relevant study aside from a few impressionistic accounts" (p. 26). For these reasons it may be useful to examine in some detail the results of that research. It should be borne in mind that that study included evaluations of the impact of regular visits as well as conjugal visits. Additionally, it is the tentative findings of that inquiry, more than any other, that are most closely related to the hypotheses and data of this study.

In examining the regular (nonconjugal) visiting patterns of wives of prisoners it was discovered that 43 percent of those spouses who visited their husbands during the first year of incarceration were no longer doing so by the second year (p. 21). It was speculated that the marital relationship may be more vulnerable than other interpersonal contacts precisely because of its more intimate nature. This seemed to be supported by the fact that prisoners' parents, siblings, and close friends all maintained a larger proportion of systematic long-term visits than did the wives of prisoners.

It was also found that the frequency of visits that a man received from his family was positively correlated with his chance of being granted parole. And once on parole a significantly greater fraction of those men remained arrest-free during their first year on the outside. The data were most revealing for return to prison during the first 12 months after release: six times as many prisoners who had had no visits were recidivists, as compared to those with consistent visits by at least three different relatives and/or friends.

Interviews were also conducted among a sample of both single and married men in order to determine how they felt about the family visiting program. Ninety percent of the men endorsed the program, including many single men who were themselves unable to participate in it. Recommendations made by prisoners reflected their desire for longer, more frequent visits, and strongly urged that common-law wives and girlfriends be made eligible for participation, especially when there were children involved (pp. 53-54).

An extremely significant discovery was the clear correlation between parole success and involvement in either the family visiting or home furlough program. Though the numbers were small, the results showed that 60 percent of the men in these programs had no problems with the law during the first year on parole, while this was true of only 42 percent of those who were not (p. 63). The full significance of this figure may be appreciated by projecting that 18 percent differential onto the more than 30,000 men presently incarcerated in California prisons.

Holt and Miller made several summary recommendations that indicated the strength of their belief in the substantive value of the family visiting program. These included making them available to common-law wives, initiating a family counseling program, placing a man in the institution nearest his home to optimize his wife's opportunity to take advantage of the program, and not allowing lack of space to be used as an excuse for limiting the extent of such programs. The authors went so far as to suggest that the social benefits to be realized from this program were such that the use of the warden's office itself should be considered when no other space seems available (p. 64)!

The report was also careful to address itself to a critical methodological question. It has been suggested that inmates motivated to maintain strong family ties with their wives and families would have special motivation to succeed on parole, thereby discounting any necessarily causal relationship between the conjugal visits and postparole success. Consequently, such men would be expected to do well even in the absence of such visits. But the data indicated that that was not so. Those with frequent family contacts had the same number of disciplinary reports, no better work records, were no more likely to be in educational and vocational programs, and were evaluated as no more promising in group counseling than nonparticipants in the family visiting program. Thus there is clear evidence for asserting a strong *independent* positive correlation between family visits and parole success.

On the basis of their study, Holt and Miller made the following bold statement: "The positive relationship between strength of family ties and success on parole has held up for 45 years of releases across very diverse offender populations and in different localities. *It is doubtful if there is any other research finding in the field of corrections which can approximate this record*" (p. 61, emphasis added).

The statement quoted above is based essentially on two previous research efforts whose results were congruent with those obtained in California. One showed that the rate of parole success went from 43 percent to 74 percent depending upon whether visits from family members were nonexistent or active and sustained (Glaser, 1964, p. 242). The other, using a huge sample drawn from a population of 17,000 men paroled over a 20 year period demonstrated a similar relationship; an excerpt of the results is indicated in Table 2-1.

The data leave little doubt that a consistent relationship has been demonstrated between the strength of family ties as expressed in frequency of visits and a man's likelihood of becoming a productive citizen after being paroled (or at least avoiding further trouble with the law) (Ohlin, 1954, p. 218).

The three studies cited above do not seem to have generated much excitement in the field of corrections. That may be due in part to their wide disparity in time, and perhaps to the fact that they were not concerned with a rehabilitation approach based on a "treatment" philosophy. And Holt and Miller were quick to remark, of their own work: "Even the strongest findings reported here suffer from a lack of replication" (p. 2). It is one of the central intentions of this book to provide just such a replication.

Table 2-1
Relationship of Family Visits to Criminal Recidivisim

Family Interest	Number of Cases	Parole Violation Rate
2-3 visits monthly	487	26%
Fewer than 1 visit monthly	1,256	47%
No visits	785	66%

Source: Reprinted by permission from L.E. Ohlin. *The Stability & Validity of Parole Experience Tables.* Doctoral Dissertation, University of Chicago, 1954.

3 Methods

In the final analysis no method can substitute for intelligence and imagination.
                                                        —Herbert Kelman (1968)

*The psychologists who are filling up the journals today just do not have the
sensitivity to human experience, and the fault lies in their training which is an
expression of what academic psychology has become.*
                                                        —Nevitt Sanford (1965)

Ernst Cassirir once said of Kurt Lewin that:

He discloses the basic character of science as the eternal attempt to go beyond
what is regarded as scientifically accessible at any specific time. To proceed
beyond the limitations of a given level of knowledge the researcher, as a rule, has
to break down the methodological taboos which condemn as "unscientific" or
"illogical" the very methods or concepts which later on prove to be basic for the
next major progress. (Cartwright, 1951)

That remark seems an appropriate preface to a discussion of the philosophical
perspective underlying the methodology and design of the present research.
Simply put the objectives of this study are twofold:

1. to provide a phenomenological account of the conjugal visiting experience
   in a prison setting, and
2. to evaluate the legitimacy of two hypotheses concerning such visits, i.e., their
   relationship to marital stability and to postparole "success."

The methods employed in this study, unlike the standard group designs for a
psychological experiment, are essentially phenomenological, naturalistic, and
nonstatistical in nature. Since this approach, while not novel, is certainly not the
usual one, it may be valuable to include some discussion of the concerns and
issues that dictated the selection of this particular style of inquiry.

The Phenomenological versus the Natural Scientific Approach

The natural sciences have historically preoccupied themselves with the study of the forces and matter of the physical world—a world whose existence and dynamic attributes are essentially independent of man. Psychology, on the other hand, as one of the social sciences, has taken as its province the study of man himself, his behavior, his experience, and his interaction with the world of things. Because of the dramatic and astonishingly rapid success of the physical sciences in the last century and a half, it has been more than a little tempting for psychologists to uncritically adopt the research paradigm responsible for the very considerable achievements that have been registered in physics, chemistry, and biology.

Gradually, however, some voices have been raised questioning the appropriateness of employing a methodology, which, while productive in one discipline, may be severely constraining in another. Eckartsberg (1971) has observed that:

The scientific method has been evolved by researchers who apply stringent criteria for control of variables, experimental manipulation, public verifiability, repeatability, and the ability to predict behavior. The realm of this scientific social psychology is characterized by being abstract, non-existential, non-situated (except in the laboratory) and group-average centered. Due to the fact of experimental isolation, complete control of circumstances, manipulation and pre-interpretation of data, and restriction of alternatives, many of the concepts and findings remain pure abstractions empty of concrete personal meaning. (P. 329)

In the face of the rigid and systematic structure of the "scientific method," what does phenomenology have to offer for a proper study of man? Perhaps little more than an unashamed respect for its own basic enterprise, namely, a presuppositionless description of direct experience. And that may turn out to be a great deal indeed. The phenomenological approach entails the acknowledgement that the *experience* and *meaning* of phenomena are as significant as the quantitative and behavioral aspects stressed by orthodox experimental research.

A phenomenological point of view holds that it is basically unsound to assume a priori that any fixed method is necessarily appropriate to a field of inquiry that is independent of the phenomenon to be investigated. Thus while rigorous measurement may be desirable in a test of serial learning or reflex speed, in other situations—i.e., an assessment of curiosity, happiness, sexual cues, or the feeling of at-homeness—one might be much more interested in qualitative data that provide a textured understanding of the meaning of the experience. There are many instances, and the present study is one, in which a phenomenological perspective would include a matrix of data some of which stresses measurement, while some centers on the personal meaning of an experience.

It is useful, in this context, to bear in mind that "research" has historically been defined as a careful search of studious inquiry, usually involving a critical and exhaustive investigation *or* experimentation intended to revise conclusions in the light of new facts. Thus, experimentation is a subset, and not coincident with research per se. With this borne in mind, one recognizes that research is a mode in which man questions the world, and the world responds according to the nature of the question. Experiments are one form of questioning, a form that prestructures the kind of answers the world can give—answers that are usually a function of some dependent variable. But even in an experiment more happens than what the experimenter is interested in. It is those residual happenings that often get left out because they do not assume quantifiable or easily categorized forms. In such instances, one may want to modify the structure of the question rather than ignore nonbehavioral, nonmeasureable (mathematically) answers.

Finally, a word on the treatment of subjects. Most often the subjects of an experiment, even human subjects, are regarded as passive, mechanistically responsive beings who produce a generally predictable spectrum to differential stimuli. But as Giorgi (1971b) has pointed out:

The subject of an experiment is not only the source of behavior, but also a source of meaning, and the meaning that a subject will impute to a situation can never be fully controlled. But this latter fact does not vitiate the scientific effort. It simply means that one has to be fully empirical and *allow the meaning of the situation for the subject to count as data* just as much as his behavior does. (p. 56, emphasis added)

Because this research project concerns itself with an experience that is novel and unique for prisoners in this country, the comment above seems particularly relevant, and a phenomenological approach most appropriate.

Naturalistic versus Experimental Research

The discussion above was devoted to the philosophical underpinnings of psychological research. The present section is more immediately concerned with the locus of research and differential methodological strategies.

Almost since the days of Titchener, laboratory experiments have been the approved of style of research in the psychological establishment. However, the European tradition of ethologists diligently engaging in field work, together with an evolving tendency toward interdisciplinary research in the social sciences, has led in the last decade to an increasing number of naturalistic studies. In the latter regard, McGuire (1967) has called for

the reduction of the currently existing walls between conventional departments, including psychology on the one hand and sociology, economics and even anthropology on the other. . . . Admittedly good fences make good neighbors, and those who wish to be in a university that is as comfortable as an old shoe, rather than to feel the zest and pain of striving for excellence through leading new intellectual advances, should stand warned that the alterations I am suggesting here would to some extent involve disturbing the peace and might also require that some old dogs learn some new tricks. (p. 236)

The new tricks to which McGuire refers may be conceptualized in the form of questions relating to the legitimacy of naturalistic studies as sufficiently "scientific" as well as to issues inherent in the use or absence of control groups and statistical procedures. It may prove valuable to examine each of these in turn.

Few would quarrel with the fact that research in naturalistic settings is less controlled than experiments done in the laboratory in the same sense that life as it is lived is more sprawling and ambiguous than systematic behavioral responses elicited under carefully controlled circumstances. But that is certainly no argument for abstaining from doing such research. On the contrary, the basic question ought to be what method of inquiry is best suited for the purpose of one's research, the nature of the questions being posed, and the limitations and constraints of the phenomenon under investigation.

Kelman (1968) put the matter in perspective by stating that "What is called for is a methodology which combines rigor and insight, verification and discovery, accuracy and empathy, replicability and human relevance. Central to this argument is a particular view of the nature of scientific analysis—a view in which "scientific" is not treated as synonymous with "rigorous" in the sense of quantitative and experimental" (p. 142). Kelman went on to emphasize that if we wish to trace the development of some pehenomenon in the setting in which it occurs, then by necessity a less rigorous, more impressionistic approach is required. This is by no means a criticism of the experimental method, but simply reflects a belief that statistical precision as an end in itself has no special value.

There is a sense in which naturalistic research needs no justification. Its raison d'être is implicit in its method. For example, Barker (in Willems and Rausch, 1969) has observed that "scientific psychology knows nothing, and can know nothing, about the real-life settings in which people live in ghettos, and suburbs, in large and small schools, in regions of poverty and affluence" (p. 31). In advancing the belief that psychology would gain much by becoming an ecobehavioral science, Barker has emphasized the importance of environment in shaping behavior, a factor often neglected in studies that view human responses as largely a function of the individual person and his intrapsychic and behavioral predispositions.

It is vital to bear in mind that techniques for solid and reliable naturalistic research are still in a state of relative infancy. For this reason, those who study behavior in special environments tend to automatically rely on the analytic perspective of the experimental method, a procedure that may very well distort and change the nature of the very phenomenon one is interested in understanding. It is unfortunate that this is so, particularly since a simple rationale for naturalistic methods is the fact that many phenomena and their correlates would not become subject to systematic inquiry at all without such methods. Perhaps Rausch (in Willems and Rausch, 1969) put it most succinctly when he remarked that naturalistic research "like other methods in science, demands training, caution and rigor, and is subject to error and limitations, but is nevertheless legitimate for scientific exploration, discovery, and even verification" (p. 144).

It may be illuminating to ask ourselves what it is about the experimental method that has historically made it so attractive to psychologists as a model of acquiring new and useful knowledge. Some few moments of introspection may be sufficient to reveal that the use of statistical tests of significance and of carefully selected control groups are surely prominent factors. And yet these were not always characteristics of psychological experiments. Boring (1954, p. 587), in analyzing all articles published in the *Journal of Experimental Psychology* over the course of a half century, discovered some very interesting patterns. The percentage of well-matched control groups included in such studies went from none in 1916 to 11 percent in 1933, and rose astronomically to 52 percent in 1951. It would not be surprising if that same journal today reflected a comparable figure in excess of 90 percent. Thus what we take for granted as a prerequisite of scholarly psychological research has been an evolutionary development that roughly parallels the admittedly remarkable achievements of the natural sciences in the past four decades.

But the obsession with clean, precise control groups may create severe limitations in naturalistic settings. Bakan (1967) has proposed that:

. . . our deep penchant for "control" of variables in our research enterprise is the facede for our penchant for mastery, not only of the variables in the limited sense in which we use this term, but in the larger sense of the control of the behavior of others. In the interests of control in research, we select such sets of alternatives which promise the greatest degree of control of the behavior of those whom we study. (P. 45)

And yet there may be situations in which much can be learned, but where strict experimental control groups are simply not feasible. The setting of the present study is one such example.

The research that forms the body of this study could not have been undertaken if strictly matched control groups had been necessary. But the impossibility of obtaining such a high standard of experimental control did not seem sufficient reason to refrain from such research altogether. Willems (in Willems and Rausch, 1969) has written squarely about the charges leveled at such research and the creativity called for under such circumstances:

Naturalistic strategies are also frequently criticized on the grounds that too seldom do they, or too seldom can they, employ proper control groups. . . the lack of explicit control over variables, the complexity of relations among variables, and absence of random assignment of subjects to research conditions in naturalistic studies often provide a loophole for other variables to crawl through. . . . The effects of passage of time, effects of variables correlated with presumed independent variables, and the equivalence of *comparison groups. . .* are but three considerations. *Appropriate control groups are serious problems for naturalistic research, but the problems should be empirically solvable through a combination of ingenuity of investigators and an understanding of the function of control groups.* (P. 59, emphasis added)

What are the implications of the foregoing comments for hypothesis testing in psychological research? Bakan (1967) has suggested that "It is when psychologists allow themselves to go beyond the scientist-subject distinction, beyond the definition of psychology purely as behavior, beyond the lower animals, beyond the presumptive regularities of laws, and beyond the restriction of research to the testing of hypotheses that discoveries concerning the nature of and functioning of the human psyche have been revealed" (p. 41).

What is especially interesting about Bakan's comments in this respect is that they rest on both mathematical *and* pragmatic considerations. He pointed out with regard to the former that the null hypothesis is almost invariably rejected when N is relatively large. In one study he conducted that included thousands of subjects throughout the United States who were administered a wide array of psychological tests, virtually every division of two groups yielded results that were statistically significant. More specifically, when subjects were divided by states, region, east or west of Mississippi, or indeed by any other criterion, the results continued to be significant. Bakan concluded that contrary to expectation, large samples showing significant differences may simply be an almost invariable result of the size of the sample whereas small samples showing significant differences may be much more indicative of real and substantive differences of effect.

The other issue is essentially utilitarian in nature, concerned with the question of "how much of a difference makes a difference." Bakan suggested that in psychological research this question cannot properly be considered outside of some practical context. Or, as he has put it, such a query immediately calls forth its implied complement, namely, "How much of a difference makes a difference *for what?*" (emphasis in original). Here the emphasis is distinction based on situational meaningfulness, rather than on simple arithmetic dissonance.

Finally, and with simple eloquence, Bakan offered an alternative to hypothesis testing as the sole means of generating worthwhile results in psychological research. He recommended:

the use of "the interocular traumatic test, [in which] you know what the data mean when the conclusion hits you between the eyes." We must overcome the myth that if our treatment of our subject matter is mathematical it is therefore precise and valid. We need to overcome the handicap associated with limited competence in mathematics, a competence that makes it possible for us to run tests of significance while it intimidates us with a vision of greater mathematical competence if only one could reach up to it. Mathematics can serve to obscure as well as to reveal. (p. 28)

The Question of Value in Psychological Research

Why do people engage in research, and particularly in psychological research? Perhaps for no reason other than that which was expressed by Aldous Huxley, who once said, "Isn't it fun to know things?" Still, researchers *do* make choices about what it is they wish to study. And all of us are acquainted with those studies about the blinking patterns of monkeys, or the effects of nodding on psychotherapeutic progress. The perspective informing this study is that although all research has potential value in enriching man's reservoir of knowledge, some investigations are more worthwhile than others. The bias of this writer is that research intended to shed some light on new ways to advance the well-being and satisfy the basic needs of human beings deserves the highest priority of public and private support.

A quote from one of psychology's foremost theoreticians speaks to this point most elegantly: "I believe that what the physical scientists have been to the world in the past, the social scientists will be to the world of the future. As the physical scientists have made it possible to modify the world to increase its habitability, the social scientists will serve. . . the commitment of men to live *with* each other in highly complex inter-relationships" (Bakan, 1965, p. 190, emphasis in original).

There is no intention here to denigrate experimental research designs in areas transparently unrelated to social problems. Rather, what is being promoted is a model of research such as that proposed by Kenneth Ring (1967) who, in referring to the work of Kurt Lewin, has observed that a subtle interplay of theory, research, and social action makes it possible for psychologists not only to further a scientific understanding of man, but to simultaneously advance human welfare.

Few have written with greater vigor about the relationship between psychological research and human problems than has Nevitt Sanford, current director of the Wright Institute in Berkeley. He has written squarely and forcefully about the issue of value in psychological inquiry, espousing the belief that:

institutes and agencies ought to encourage psychologists to study problems that people really worry about rather than only problems formulated on the basis of reading the professional journals. . . . [Psychologists] would be stimulated to devise methods for solving problems rather than continuing themselves, as they do today, to [study] problems to which existing methods are suited (Sanford, 1965, p. 192).

Sanford minced no words in indicting researchers who are extremely adept at defining variables, formulating hypotheses, designing precise experiments, manipulating data statistically, and getting their work published, all without any sensitive appreciation of the fact that their subjects are flesh and blood persons. He argued a fundamental shift of posture in psychological research, insisting that the kind of approach needed for an understanding of human problems is of a different sort than that which guides laboratory research. Whereas the latter tends to be formal, mechanistic, specialized, and concrete, the former would be dynamic, holistic, comprehensive, and as abstract as suited the problem at hand.

In addition to his comments on research approaches, Sanford also has emphasized the need for more solid studies in naturalistic social settings, especially those that have been designed to modify people's behavior in some way such as schools, hospitals, psychotherapeutic programs, and correctional institutions. He acknowledged that such environments will require a delicate blend of sociological analysis and individual psychological change.

All of what has been said thus far in this chapter is intended to provide a solidly grounded case for research that is conducted in a naturalistic setting with a phenomenological approach, and where the issues of human value and potential social action are mainsprings for doing such research at all. If the present study falls short of the model of research outlined above, it will at least have demonstrated the feasibility of attempting an investigation predicated more on what seems worthwhile for the future condition of man than what can be shown to be significant at the .01 level.

The fact of the matter is that any study that takes place within the confines of a prison in this country must operate with considerable handicaps, both administrative and methodological. On several occasions as the collection of data was in progress, it seemed reasonable to give up the whole enterprise because of what seemed insurmountable hurdles—limited access to subjects, questions regarding inmate reliability, the problem of obtaining a well-matched control group, transfer and release of subjects, suspicion regarding the researcher's motivation, and a welter of difficulties related to variables that wouldn't stay fixed. In the final analysis, it was decided to proceed in such a way as to test Sanford's belief that "testing hypotheses in natural environments would clarify their relevance to the real world and provide directions for social action" (p. 126).

The Setting

The setting for this research was Soledad Prison, officially known as the Correctional Training Facility for Men at Soledad. Located in the center of the Salinas Valley, it is surrounded by the rolling farmlands of Monterey County and the slopes of the Santa Lucia Mountains. The prison sits somewhat incongruously among the patchwork of alfalfa and corn fields, an alien structure, still despised by a good number of local townspeople who opposed its construction from the outset.

Soledad was built in the late 1940s and early 1950s through a state appropriation of more than $10 million. Planned as a "model prison" in what was to be an era of penal reform inaugurated by then Governor Earl Warren, it includes lovely floral walkways, baseball diamonds, gymnasiums, golf course, movie theaters, classrooms, and individual cells. Originally intended to accommodate 1,500 men, the current population is about 3,200.

The entire institution is divided into three separate areas designated as the "North," "Central," and "South" facilities, respectively. The research for the present study took place exclusively at the South and Central sectors of the penitentiary. South facility houses about 400 men, all of whom have minimum custody status and live in dormitorylike structures similar to military barracks. The atmosphere is considerably more relaxed than the rest of the prison, with men either working at regular jobs (usually on the land) or sitting in threes and fours smoking and involved in conversation. Still, there are the starkly erected guntowers and fencing around the security area to remind one that this is a prison.

Central facility is an entirely different setting. It is there that prisoners such as Sirhan Sirhan and Juan Corona are detained in maximum custody, an area that includes protective custody for those whose lives have been threatened by other inmates because of gang affiliation, "snitching" (informing), or accumulating impossibly high gambling debts. Central also includes close custody prisoners, those who have violated some institutional regulation or have been caught smuggling in some contraband, and who will be carefully observed for a number of months, usually until the authorities feel comfortable that they are once again cooperative and compliant. The noise approaches deafening proportions and the echo of footsteps, talking, yelling, the jangle of keys, and the metallic clanging of doors opening and closing is bleakly oppressive to the newcomer.

The Selection of Subjects

Initially, an attempt was made to do this research at another state prison closer to the Bay Area—Deuell Vocational Institute (also known as D.V.I.), located in Tracy, California. A meeting with a staff person there revealed that the family visiting program was very small in scope, and that participating inmates had such visits on the average of once every five months. Because of the infrequency of the visits (hardly a significant intervention at that rate) and the limited number of men from whom a sample could be drawn, D.V.I. was dropped as a potential site of this research.

A call to the department of corrections in Sacramento revealed that Soledad had the most extensive family visiting program in the state. A letter to the superintendent was quickly responded to and extensive cooperation offered. The investigator was met at Soledad by Mr. Derral Byers, the counselor who coordinated the visiting program for all of South facility. He was to prove an invaluable liaison throughout the research period.

The original intention was to identify two groups of 20 men each—those who had conjugal visits with their wives fairly regularly, and a matched control group who saw their wives only on ordinary visits. This was no simple task. First of all, there was no central roster indicating which men received family visits and which of these took place with wives rather than parents, siblings, or children. Second, the frequency of such visits was only every two and a half or three months for all medium custody prisoners and for about 40 percent of the minimum custody men (Minimum A status). Only prisoners classified as Minimum B received such visits with their wives fairly often—every 30 days or so. (See Chapter 4 for further details on the relationship of classification to family visiting.)

Of 120 men who had Minimum B status in May 1975, ten were restricted because of sex offenses, many did not have family visits at all, and of those who did, a fair number did not include wives. A systematic search of the daily visiting log (the only document that indicated who was visited and whether or not the visit was a regular one or a family visit) revealed that 30 men of Minimum B status had had conjugal visits at least once. Of those, 20 were selected on the basis of having had at least three such visits in the past four months.

The next order of business was to attempt to obtain a reasonably well-matched control group since the pivotal thrust of the research was to analyze the differential effects of conjugal versus ordinary visits. This proved a formidable business since it became evident rather quickly that such a group just did not exist at the prison. Ideally, it would have been necessary to locate 20 men with Minimum B custody status of comparable ages, ethnic backgrounds, crimes committed, and time served who saw their wives only on regular visits. The problem was that all men with such custody status were eligible for conjugal visits as soon as their names came up on the waiting list—perhaps two to three months after achieving such status.

Part of the solution lay in locating seven men in South facility who had Minimum B status, were married, and had applied for family visits, but whose first such visit had not yet occurred. The balance of the men had to be selected from other segments of the prison population, the majority of whom had committed more serious offenses, many of whom were unmarried, or whose wives did not visit them regularly or at all for a variety of reasons. It required weeks of searching through records to find the additional 13 men, all of whom were housed in Central facility: two in close custody, and 11 in protective custody. These men, by virtue of their custody status, are not allowed family (including conjugal) visits for security reasons. Thus there was now a pool of 20 married inmates who could not be said to constitute a true "control group" because they could not be tightly matched for the variables described above. But it was considered a useful "comparison group" in Willems' (in Willems and Rausch, 1969) sense of that term. At that point, the interviewing began.

Characteristics of the Experimental and Comparison Groups

The experimental group consisted of 20 prisoners who had received at least three conjugal visits from their wives in the past four months. The comparison group consisted of 20 prisoners who had received ordinary, but not conjugal, visits from their wives. They could not be matched on the basis of the sector of the prison in which they were housed, their custody status, or on an *individual* basis for age, ethnic background, time served, and number of years married. *But* striking parallels were demonstrated when they were viewed as groups (see Table 3-1). The difference in years of marriage for men who received conjugal visits is in large part accounted for by three men in that group who were married for 25, 29, and 30 years, respectively. In the comparison group, no inmate had had a marriage of over 20 years duration.

Examination of the criminal offenses for which the subjects were incarcerated revealed that they include robbery, burglary, manslaughter, murder, forgery, and kidnapping *for both groups.* Rape was the only crime committed by an inmate in one group but not the other. It is also useful to bear in mind that while 13 subjects in the comparison group lived in a different section of the prison, the remaining seven came from South facility, from which all of the experimental subjects were selected.

Thus, for all its methodological shortcomings in terms of a rigorously well-matched control group, it is felt that the comparison group demonstrated sufficient equivalence on the variables discussed above to merit acceptance for purposes of the present research.

Data Collection

Initially there was some equivocation as to whether it would be more valid to use a questionnaire or an interview in order to gather data. Since the issue of sex was a central one, it was initially thought that a questionnaire might be less threatening and result in more reliable information. On the other hand, an interview seemed to offer more opportunity for subtlety and nuance with

Table 3-1
Characteristics of Subjects in Two Different Prison Visiting Programs

Type of Visit	Mean Age	Mean Years Married	Ethnicity
Ordinary	31	6.5	12 white
			5 black
			3 Mexican-American
Conjugal	35	8.8	11 white
			5 black
			4 Mexican-American

respect to a subject often fraught with anxiety, dishonesty, guilt, and shame. A number of sources were helpful in making decisions related to the collection of data.

Selltiz et al (1964) point out that each of the aforementioned methods has its assets and liabilities. Supporting the use of the questionnaire, they noted the following advantages: may be mailed, can be administered to large numbers simultaneously, no pressure for an immediate response, confidence in guaranteed anonymity, and the fact that standardized instructions ensure uniformity of comprehension. The interview, on the other hand, derives its special value essentially because of its flexibility. One may repeat and rephrase questions, ask for elaborations, notice *how* an answer is given besides *what* it happens to be, etc. Interviews are also preferred for eliciting information about complex, emotion-laden subjects. One has the possibility in an interview situation of encouraging freedom and honesty of expression by creating an atmosphere that permits respondents to discuss feelings or behaviors that are not necessarily endorsed by the culture at large.

Hence, it was ultimately decided to double the assets by using both—that is, a questionnaire that would serve as a basic framework for a loosely structured interview. It was structured in that each *set* of subjects was asked the same questions in the same sequence, but it was loose in the sense that some responses generated further questions which, while relevant, were not actually part of the original protocol.

Item Generation

Free-form brainstorming was responsible for the first rough draft of the questionnaire. Though two specific hypotheses were to be tested, the questionnaire was mainly intended as a way of eliciting information about the *meaning* of the experience of conjugal visits. So it was that there were items regarding space, privacy, feeling states, involvement of children, wife's comfort, sexual anxiety, sexual pleasure, effects on the marriage and others, both experiential and evaluative in nature. Copies of this initial compilation were sent to the superintendent of Soledad and his deputies, the director of research for the department of corrections in Sacramento, and to Dr. Norman Holt, a penologist in Southern California and the only other person who has done research on family visits in this state. Their comments and criticism led to subsequent modifications. Finally, the revised questionnaire was given a trial run through the cooperation of the Delancey Street Foundation in San Francisco which made available several ex-convicts who agreed to be interviewed. The feedback from these men resulted in further changes, and the final version of the questionnaire forms Appendix B.

Method of Interviewing

It is no easy thing to interview people about sexual aspects of their lives, and the problem is compounded when the subjects are prisoners. Men in prison tend to be boastful and stereotypic in speaking about sexual experiences. Additionally, all outsiders are suspect, especially the benign researcher to whom prisoners will often tell anything they believe might tend to ameliorate their situation. It was vital, then, to develop a style of interviewing that minimized these pitfalls.

Kinsey et al (1948) were of invaluable assistance in that regard. The authors of that first monumental study of sexuality in the human male discovered some simple rules of thumb when interviewing about sexual matters. Since they spoke with everyone from pimp and prisoner to student and professional, they found it useful to be acquainted with the jargon and special vocabulary of these sub-groups. Suspending value judgments, being surprised at nothing they heard no matter how bizarre, probing only when timely, returning to questions when more rapport was established, and having a friendly, open, and interested demeanor also proved helpful. So did the interviewer's degree of comfort with his own sexuality and ease of asking others about theirs. These were all guidelines that proved extremely valuable in interviewing the men at Soledad; so much so that, at times, subjects volunteered information that had been omitted from the questionnaire because it had been regarded as too intimate!

Data Analysis

The analysis of data for this research had two basic components. The first had to do with evaluating whether or not the hypotheses advanced in Chapter 1 were confirmed or not. The second was concerned with examining the differences in meaning and experience between conjugal visits and ordinary visits as described by the inmates who participated in these two programs, respectively.

Testing the Two Major Hypotheses

The first hypothesis was that participation in conjugal visits has a positive effect on parole outcome. The criteria that were to assess whether or not that is the case were based on classifications suggested by Holt and Miller (1972). Thus, each man in both groups was placed in one of three categories after a one year followup. These were:

1. *no parole difficulties*: no known arrests or violations;
2. *minor difficulties*: arrests without convictions, misdemeanor convictions, fines, absconding from supervision;

3. *serious difficulties*: return to prison as a result of parole violation or new felony commitments.

If the subject was still in prison, the criterion used was the number and type of disciplinary reports incurred for the 12 month period subsequent to the initial interview. Given the small numbers of men in the groups, contrasts were based on gross percentages of subjects in each of the three groups.

The second hypothesis was that participation in conjugal visits is conducive to marital stability. Here the criteria used were whether or not the subject was still married, divorced, or separated. Additionally, each subject was asked if there were any serious problems that he was currently experiencing in his marriage; and if so, what they were. Here, too, a percentage comparison was utilized, as well as a more impressionistic assessment of the nature of the problems described as existing in the relationship (see Appendix B).

Contrast of Conjugal Visiting versus Ordinary Visiting Experience in Prison

The attempt here was to evaluate the differential psychological, social, and sexual benefits that were derived from conjugal, as opposed to ordinary, visits. In this regard, the following factors were contrasted, not statistically, but rather in terms of felt experiences:

1. frequency of visits,
2. suitability of visiting areas,
3. sense of privacy,
4. prisoner's state of mind during visit,
5. attitude toward others after visit,
6. involvement of prisoner's children,
7. prisoner's treatment of wife during visit, and
8. plans regarding parole in context of visit.

Additionally, there was an analysis of some other issues, mainly sexual in nature, which did not lend themselves to contrast but which applied exclusively to the conjugal visits. These included the following:

1. relative significance of sex during visits,
2. degree of anxiety regarding sexual "performance,"
3. sexual responsiveness of wife,
4. degree of sexual pleasure compared to home setting,
5. evaluation of effect of conjugal visit on marriage,
6. attitude toward conjugal visits for single men and those with common-law wives,

7. most important benefit of conjugal visit,
8. presumed motivation of California Department of Corrections in initiating conjugal visits, and
9. value of conjugal visits relative to any other program available in the institution.

It was hoped that the data analysis described above would serve the twin purposes of determining the degree to which two critically significant psychosocial hypotheses were warranted, as well as providing a meaningful description of one of the most unique experiences in our nation's prisons: the conjugal visit.

4

The Family Visiting Program at Soledad

This chapter represents an attempt to provide a descriptive account of the family visiting program at the Soledad Correctional Training Facility. It will include a brief commentary on its historical development, an indication of its scope and operation, and a comparative description of the regular visiting areas versus the family visiting accommodations. Finally, the transcript of an interview with an inmate and his wife will be offered, an exchange that took place between the couple and this writer during the course of one of their family visits.

History of the Program

The following excerpt regarding the development of the family visiting program in California's prisons was taken from a pamphlet issued by the state corrections department in 1972:

The idea of private visits by wives of inmates was long a subject of discussion and controversy among the nation's prison authorities. California's Department of Corrections had studied the possibility of conjugal visits during the mid-1960's, but no action resulted. The idea got the impetus it needed in 1968, however, when Governor Ronald Reagan suggested to department officials that they should give it a try . . . at the California Correctional Institution at Tehachapi.
. . . The visits of up to two days were permitted for legal wives, children, parents, and other immediate family members. The Tehachapi program was started in two attractively furnished cottages, buildings no longer used as staff housing. . . . Family visiting started without special funding by the state legislature.
    The Tehachapi program did not place emphasis on providing a sexual outlet. It was not viewed primarily as a force against prison homosexuality, a chronic problem in confinement facilities. Instead, the program was regarded as an attempt to help inmates retain family ties which might sustain them following release from prison.
    The pilot program at Tehachapi was judged a success in a department evaluation in early 1971. Other institutions were instructed to start the program, but again without adding money to the state budget. (California Dept. of Corrections, 1972)

One may observe several interesting things about the statements noted above. Perhaps the most noticeable is the clear desire on the part of the California Department of Corrections (CDC) to distinguish family visits from conjugal visits per se. The sexual intimacy afforded during such visits with wives is explicitly dismissed as being a major motivation for the program's inception, as is its possible usefulness in reducing the incidence of homosexual assaults. Rather, one is told that the intent of this new program is to promote the continuity of strong family ties that may subsequently provide significant support systems for prisoners after their release.

Additionally, the department points out that the program materialized not through legislative action, nor with any state funding assistance, but through executive recommendation, and the creative improvisation of both penal administration and inmate labor. What is especially noteworthy is that, despite the patchwork nature of the program, it was deemed a success after being in effect for only two years — a remarkable achievement in the field of corrections.

The Family Visiting Program at Soledad

The belief that sex is only an incidental issue in family visits is belied by recent statistics from Soledad's program. During the last quarter of 1975 there were a total of 487 family visits. Of these, 333 were from wives only, or wives accompanied by children. The remainder consisted of visits from parents, children only, siblings and, much less frequently, from aunts, uncles, and grand-parents (*Soledad . . . Memorandum,* 1975). When more than two-thirds of all such visits include a man's wife, it becomes clear that, while not an exclusive factor, the sexual one is prominent and vital, and understandably so.

It is also of paramount importance to bear in mind the time element differentiating conjugal visits from ordinary visits. The former, averaging 43 hours, last more than ten times as long as the latter, whose duration is customarily three to four hours.

The frequency of family visits at Soledad also reflects the considerable extent to which custody status affects how often an inmate can expect these visits with his wife. These respective frequencies are shown in Table 4-1 and represent the average length of waiting time between visits after a man's name has been placed on the visiting calendar.

Table 4-1
Relationship of Custody Status to Frequency of Family Visits

Custody Classification	*Interval Between Family Visits*
Maximum	No family visits
Protective	No family visits
Medium A	3 months
Medium B	3 months
Minimum A	3 months
Minimum B	4-6 weeks

Description of the Visiting Facilities

A brief description of the respective visiting areas used by the different groups of subjects in this study will provide a context within which one may better appreciate just how special are the sites afforded prisoners for conjugal visits. The several facilities described below range from the most to the least restrictive.

Protective Custody Visiting Area

The entire space is 6 by 18 feet. At any one time, there is room for six visitors who communicate with relatives through a thick glass partition by telephone. Each visitor has an area about three feet wide in which he sits for the duration of the visit. One dim fluorescent lamp lights the entire area. Because the visitors do not have separate cubicles, they are exposed to all conversations taking place simultaneously. The attempt to overcome this cacaphony of clashing exchanges leads visitors to raise their voices, which simply compounds the noise overload. The crying of children who have no place in which to freely move about further exacerbates the situation.

During the afternoon hours, the sun shines directly on the plate glass partition for long periods of time, thereby preventing visitors and prisoners from seeing each other clearly. There is a sense of continual frustration and impersonality in which both parties strain through a veil of physical discomfort and omnipresent barriers to make at least a semblance of human contact. Perhaps most painful is the absolute inability of a visitor to ever touch an inmate. Some men have been seeing their wives under these circumstances for several years. The emotional consequences of such visitations will be discussed in the next chapter.

Close Custody Visiting Area

This area provides a marked contrast to the one just described. It is a fairly large and spacious room, measuring about 25 by 70 feet. There are chairs and tables throughout, although the latter, being only two feet high (to prevent contraband from being passed underneath them), give the appearance of a grade school lunchroom. There are several vending machines from which prisoners and their relatives and friends may purchase candy, soda, hot beverages, and soup. The room can easily accommodate in excess of 100 people, and often does.

All visitors must pass through a metal detector. Men are asked to empty their pockets and women to expose the contents of their purses. No food or gifts may be brought in, although photographs and legal documents are allowed.

Inmates and their female visitors are told that they may kiss each other only on entering and leaving, and that discreet embracing and hand holding are permissable. Prisoners soon learn what the various threshhold points of the different guards are with respect to the degree and frequency of touching with their wives. The officers state that from time to time visits are immediately terminated due to attempts at intercourse and oral sex, mainly behind the vending machines.

Probably the most severe limitation here is the lack of access to the outside, especially when young children are involved, who often get restless after short periods indoors. Plans are currently being discussed to remedy this by arranging for outside patio visiting, as well as for evening visits.

Minimum Custody Visting Area

This is an L-shaped separate cottagelike area about 40 feet square. It is well lit, with eight small wooden tables and about 30 metal frame chairs. It is not nearly as crowded as the close custody visiting room, with only a dozen or so people using it on weekdays and three to four times that amount on weekends. One officer is usually present most of the time, but the atmosphere is one of relative informality. There is the sense there that a man and his visitor may create a small zone of quasi-privacy if there is not an overflow of visitors that day.

The major asset of this setting is that the cottage opens onto an outside lawn area containing 17 picnic tables. This area is patroled by two guards and ob-served by the officer in the guntower a few yards away. Visitors may elect to stay indoors or out at will, although from October to February the rains often prevent outdoor visits. Again, the issue of touching one's wife or girlfriend is a sensitive one. However, the boundaries appear less stringent here unless they are flagrantly abused. When that happens, the penalty may be immediate term-ination of the visit.

Family Visiting Facilities

These are the accommodations used for conjugal visits and for visits with other members of the prisoner's immediate family. The vast majority of men eligible for such visits use one of ten trailers acquired (mainly through donations) for that purpose. But a small fraction of married men, numbering between 30 and 40, whose custody classification is Minimum B, are allowed visits in one of two apart-ments on the grounds that were formerly used for staff housing. A brief description of each of these follows.

The Trailers. The ten trailers are spread throughout the institution, with one

allotted to South facility, the minimum custody sector of the prison. The
condition of these trailers varies considerably, from very old and in need of
extensive repairs to a few nearly new ones. The one inspected by this writer
was one of the latter. It consisted of a kitchen, living room, two bedrooms,
and a modern tiled bathroom. The kitchen contains a formica table, four
chairs, a new refrigerator, modern gas range and oven, cabinets, plates, cups,
saucers, frying pan, forks, spoons, and plastic knives, and one steak knife
chained to the wall above the counter space.

The living room is nicely carpeted and has a couch, coffee table, easy
chair, television set, and clock radio. The bedrooms, while somewhat small,
contain clothes closets, small dressers, and a night table. Once inside, the
only reminder that one is on prison grounds is the site of the guntower 20 feet
away, visible from the kitchen window.

The Apartments. The two apartments are attached to one another and are
separated by a short corridor, which guarantees the privacy of the two families
using them. Though less modern than the newest of the trailers, the individual
rooms are all considerably larger.

Both apartments open onto a large common lawn for family use—an
area convenient for kids to play in as well as for family picnics. The apartments
are located across the street from the visitors' parking lot and adjacent to the
guest quarters used mainly by CDC officials. What is most interesting about
this is that the apartments, unlike the trailers, are not situated within the
security perimeter. Thus, it is theoretically possible and quite simple for an
inmate to walk the few hundred yards off the prison grounds without being
detected. However, the high regard in which this program is held by the men
is such that only one prisoner has escaped during the five years of its operation.

What is important to note in comparing these different facilities is the
extent to which they simulate the conditions of normality beyond prison
walls. In the protective custody area, the circumstances and setting necessarily
cause more anguish than joy. The integrity and basic humanity of both the
prisoner and his visitor are sharply reduced by the inability to ever touch each
other, and the constant strain—to hear what is said and to see one another clearly
through the glare of the sun. This maddening confinement and absolute lack
of privacy often conspire to make the visit more painful than no visit at all.
This unfortunate fact will be documented in Chapter 5.

The subsequent visiting facilities described are progressively more humane.
Larger space, greater freedom of movement, better illumination, access to the
outdoors, availability of snacks, etc. all tend to create an atmosphere in which
the captive state of the inmate is temporarily reduced, and where it becomes
possible for the visit to truly alleviate the abiding loneliness and solitude of
incarceration.

A Prisoner and His Wife Talk About Conjugal Visits

In the course of obtaining data for this research study, it seemed worthwhile to
supplement the testing of particular hypotheses with at least a partial account
of the experience of the conjugal visit by the inmate participants and their wives.
To that end, men who agreed to be interviewed for the study were asked to consider whether they would feel comfortable allowing the researcher to spend a
couple of hours with them during the course of a future family visit. Several
were receptive, and ultimately a couple was selected, mainly on the basis of
having been involved in the program at Soledad since its inception in 1971.
Authorization was secured from prison officials, who by this time knew the researcher well enough to approve even this somewhat unorthodox request.

Shortly thereafter, this writer had the opportunity to spend approximately
two and a half hours with Jim, his wife, Karen, and their ten year old son,
Robert (ficticious names have been substituted), at the beginning and end of
their family visit on January 15-17, 1976. During this period, they were informally interviewed regarding several aspects of their experience in the program.
Their responses were taped, and an edited transcript appears below.[a]

A few words concerning general background information and observations
during the course of the interview may be pertinent here. Jim had been one of
the original subjects in the experimental group—a young man in his late twenties who had been sentenced to life for a major felony eight years ago. He
comes before the parole board in 1976. His wife visited him at Soledad regularly
for the first two years, and then in 1971, when family visits began at Soledad,
they were among the first participants. It is important to note that before those
visits were instituted, Jim was regarded as a chronic behavior problem by prison
officials. By his own admission, he was "pretty loose," given to impulsive acts
and systematically uncooperative with institutional regulations. Since the family
visits began, it would be no exaggeration to say that his state of being has changed
radically. That is not simply a matter of self-report, but is corroborated by the
superintendent of Soledad and the associate superintendent who administers
South facility where Jim lives.

The visit was striking in several respects. It was the first time in eight months
of seeing Jim fairly regularly that he appeared to be totally relaxed, even playful.
He did not have to be deferential to guards, alert and sensitive to prison routine
(work, meals, lights out, picking up subtle cues of potential danger, etc.), or
careful about his behavior with his wife, as he would have on ordinary visits. He
pointed out that sitting in a soft easychair was a special experience, while Karen
commented on the opportunity to do simple things like turning lights on and
off, something a prisoner never does under regular circumstances.

But the deepest impression of the time spent with Jim and his wife was of
the natural warmth and tenderness that flowed between them, the currents of

---

[a]This interview is reprinted by permission.

affection and commitment borne of time and a shared struggle. One was startled at the "strangeness" of a marital relationship flowering in the midst of an environment customarily associated with brutality and inhumanity. The interview began with Karen bringing in a cup of coffee for Jim; the two of them answered questions put to them in a leisurely fashion, with Karen sitting on a pillow beside Jim, maintaining a gentle contact with him throughout:

Interviewer: Karen, you said the very first hours of the first family visit you had were uncomfortable. Could you say something about what that was like?

Karen: It was terrible for me. I don't know, Jim even said to me "What's the matter, don't you like me?" I had been away from him for so long—for two years. I mean I was seeing him in the visiting room, but there was no physical contact. And all of a sudden we were together. And after he said that to me I was able to talk to him and tell him how I was feeling. All of a sudden everything bam!—it was like Jim was a new person.

Jim: She had found out a lot about me in two years without having any intimate contact. I was insane when I was out before and I imagine it scared her a lot and I imagine she hoped I had changed and didn't know how much I *had* changed.

Karen: It wasn't just that. I was just afraid of so many things. I didn't know if you still wanted me or would feel pleased with me—just the whole things.... And then Jim was coming on really strong to me and—

Jim: Well I hadn't done anything for two years!!

Karen: I know it, I know it, but it really kind of freaked me. But then after that it was really nice.

Jim: And so you worked out whatever tensions existed during the course of that visit.

Karen: Yeah, I think so.

Interviewer: You mentioned, Jim, when I first spoke with you, that the time spent with Karen in the visiting room just prior to the family visit in the apartment is a strain for the two of you. Would you say something about why that's so?

Jim: Knowing that you're going to the apartments and thinking about how quickly we'll be able to get out there, and anticipating any number of problems in the prison, a possible lock-down, cancellation of visits, you never know what's going to happen, so we're always anxious to get to the apartment. Plus, you know you can't really relax there in the visiting room. Like here, Karen can sit down, we can talk, Robert's occupied....

Karen: Yeah, it seems silly to spend our time sitting there and having our movements restricted when actually we're here to be here.

Interviewer: So you didn't ever experience that having the additional time was valuable because it was under relatively strained circumstances?

Jim: That time just doesn't mean as much to us.

Karen: I guess we're just anxious to be alone together.

Interviewer: What effect does having to report for counts have on the time you spend with your family? (Note: Prisoners on family visits must walk to the guntower for counts at 8:00 A.M., 11:30 A.M., 4:30 P.M., and there is a 9:30 P.M. count that involves an officer knocking at the door to check out the prisoner).

Karen (laughing): Oh, we all go with him, we all go together.

Jim: Not in the mornings you don't! I'm always conscious of it. It's a big thing. Like right now you just made me snap—I'm wondering what time it is. It's something I like to get over with. Yeah, I don't like the counts. It's not so much that it reminds me I'm in prison; it's that I have to be someplace. You know, I can't sit down, relax, start eating—everything has to be based around the count.

Karen: That's funny. I'm totally unaware of it except for the 9:30 evening count. I'm very aware of that one. You know, I'm waiting at nine o'clock and I'm saying to Jim—What time is it? What time is it?

Jim: I try to engineer what we do around the counts. I won't start anything I can't finish before the count.

Interviewer: You've said that during family visits you can be a husband and father. How, in any way, are those roles restricted or different from when you were on the outside? Also, have the visits changed how you relate to your wife and son in any particular ways?

Jim: Well, the first thing that comes to mind is my son. You know, you can't relate to your son as a father in two days a month. You have to be around him to relate to his problems, his needs—so I feel inadequate in that respect. No so much with Karen.

Interviewer: Have you noticed any advantages to your son from family visits as opposed to when he came during regular visiting time?

Karen: Oh yes!

Jim: Just being able to play basketball with him and talk with him and work with his school work with him makes a big difference.

Interviewer: It sounds like there's an incredible contrast between the feeling of the family visit and the ordinary ones.

Jim: Oh yeah! For the two years that we had only ordinary visits I think the only way my son could relate to me was I was the one saying to him, "Sit down! Be cool!" because the officers don't like it when a kid makes a lot of noise or moves around too much. I didn't like doing it. I used to tell Karen, "I'm just like a guard to him."

Karen: Also there's space and time on family visits for us to separate and then come together—something that's not really possible on a regular visit.

Interviewer: What's been the impact on your son of his father being in prison? What does he say at home about the visits or about his Dad in general?

Karen: Well, we were very honest with him even in the very beginning. He knew what was happening. So rather than keep it from him we just let him know things as they happened. Difficulties have been coming up in school. Teachers have said in conferences with me usually at the beginning of the year that they've had to step in when other kids would tease him, saying "Yer old man's in jail" or something like that. Now Robert's handled it fairly well on most occasions. But the funny thing is the kids whose fathers are cops get it too—"Oh, yer old man's a pig."

Interviewer: I would think that kind of teasing would ease up as Robert goes into higher grades.

Karen: Maybe, but then he's quite sensitive about it. He's on the basketball team at school, and I asked him a few days ago, "Did you tell your coach you wouldn't be here for the game Friday but you would Saturday?" He says, "No, I haven't said anything to him." And I say, "Well, why don't you?" And he says, "Well, I don't know what to say." I say, "Just say you're going out of town, " and he says, "No, he might ask me where, and I don't want to have to explain it." So he's sensitive about it. But at other times he'll open up to me. If he sees that I'm down he'll say, "Is it Dad?" and I'll say, "Yeah, I'm missing him," and he'll say, "I miss him too," and he'll air his feelings with me.

Interviewer: Could you say whether during the course of the visits your relationship to each other has changed either emotionally or in terms of your roles as husband and wife?

Jim: Well, I used to be pretty loose, and Karen's life style has blossomed. She was really confined before and now she's changed in ways that I can really appreciate and I've toned down on my demands and overbearing style. I'm not that way anymore. I'll do a lot of things now that I wouldn't do before like household things.

Karen: And enjoy doing them.

Jim: Yeah, and enjoy them.

Karen: It was nice the way it happened.

Interviewer: Jim, are you ever conflicted about whether you're giving more time and attention to your wife rather than your son or vice-versa?

Jim: Yeah, that bothers me sometimes.

Karen: Well, we have our time together and Robert is very understanding. He knows that there's time when we want to be alone and respects that; he doesn't bother us and he knows when we're finished with our time that we give time to him—off to the basketball courts or whatever.

Jim: Sometimes I feel though that I don't give him enough time. And a lot of times I feel that I'm too abrupt or short-tempered with him because I wanna do something else.

Karen: But I enjoy watching the two of you go off together, you know.

Jim: Also, it's his choice now whether he even wants to come down or not to visit with Karen, or to come down a day later with a friend.

Interviewer: Is that all right with you?

Jim: Oh yeah, it was my idea. Also the purpose of that isn't so much for she and I to have time together although that's groovy; it's that I think he's missing too much school—two days every month.

Karen: Yes, his teachers have said that too.

Interviewer: What kinds of comments have staff people made to you regarding your family visits?

Jim: It depends on the officers. It's as varied as you could imagine. Some of them are very glad that it's happening like Mr. Peterson, and tend to see all the positive factors, and other ones see only the sexual aspect of it, and then there's others who think the whole thing is negative and has no value.

Interviewer: What would you say to critics of the family visiting program who contend that if a man has committed a crime, and is being punished, why should he be allowed intimate contact with his wife?

Jim: I'm being punished. O.K., I got that coming. But what about them? They have rights too.

Interviewer: And how would you answer the objection that that may be true, that your wife and child don't deserve to be punished, but while a program like this operates you obviously derive some benefits from it as well, the feeling being that you don't offer an opportunity of this sort to a man who's being punished?

Jim: I don't agree that I should be punished to the extent that I'm denied any pleasures. I don't believe that society benefits from my losing whatever family contacts are possible. If anything it would be a detriment because I'd have even less to care about when I got out. If I didn't have a family to care about it would be very easy to get in trouble again.

Interviewer: The Philippines and Mexico have prison colonies where a man's wife and family may live with him in separate cottages. What would you think of that kind of idea being implemented in a place like Soledad, if the families of such men were receptive to it?

Jim: I think the Scandinavian view is more realistic than that. A man is permitted weekend passes at the family home and you work and support your family all week and return to prison at night. I'm more interested in supporting an involvement of the prisoner in the community than isolating him in a certain area. My idea of what corrections could be would be to confine me to my house and my job, and have people check on me regularly so that I'd always have to be at work or at the house.

Interviewer: Isn't that similar to the present work furlough program?

Jim: Yeah, but why limit it to the last four months of a guy's sentence? Why not do that kind of thing for five years if necessary?

Interviewer: You've mentioned that there's a particular juncture during the visit when you and Karen both begin to feel depression realizing that the visit is approaching its end. I wonder if you could say something about that and at what point it seems to happen?

Karen: The night before the final day. And then there's always the last morning when we try to busy ourselves. We see each other, we pass each other and tend to avoid direct eye contact.

Interviewer: So that last morning seems rough and it doesn't seem to change over time—like you've had these visits about five years now.

Karen: No, no it doesn't.

Interviewer: Do you think there's anything that might be done to improve the functioning of the family visiting program as it exists now other than making it more frequent?

Jim: Alleviating some of the count times would help from my point of view.

Karen: We try to make it valuable for each other. It's hard to say what they could or couldn't do.

Jim: I could see them doing a lot of little things.

Karen: Sure, but they're not important, at least not to me.

Interviewer: Karen, there were a few things I wanted to ask you that come out of the responses to the questionnaire I'd sent to you and one of them has to do with your feelings after the visit's ended. There was something you wrote that seemed to suggest that's a fairly painful time. Could you say something about what your emotional state is like after you've left Jim?

Karen: It's difficult to put in words . . . it really is difficult. It's like we come together here and then we're torn apart, and each time it's extremely difficult. It's not loneliness. It's just leaving Jim here. That's what hurts . . . and given a few miles on the road I get myself together, but I wish I could have more control.

Interviewer: Do you remember your reaction when Jim told you that this kind of program was going to be initiated?

Karen: We felt real good about it. One of the things on our first visit that I was thinking about was, wow, it's the first time in two years that Jim's turned lights on and off, and a lot of other things like that which he simply hadn't done in a long time.

Jim: Preparing your own food's really strange and being able to eat any time you want. And a bathtub is really a trip too. We have only showers.

Karen: Even opening up doors.

Interviewer: You mean because doors and gates are always opened for you, usually electronically?

Jim: Yeah, right. And the refrigerator. Being able to cook, to heat your own water. Glasses, cups, mugs. I can't even go into it. All the different little things. Chairs, like I don't sit on chairs like this [soft easy chair] anywhere except here. They're all metal folding chairs.

Interviewer: I'm wondering if either one of you wants to say anything about your experience in the program that you think people ought to know about, particularly those who may have stereotyped pictures of what it's like.

Karen: Well, a lot of my friends at work think it's wonderful.

Interviewer: So you haven't heard any negative comments about it?

Karen: No, not about family visits, but I've had negative feelings expressed when people find out my husband's in prison, which they seem to accept, but when they find out that I've been with him for as long as I have or that I'm supporting him and standing behind him they think it's strange. Some of them say, "What're you doing that for? You're wasting your life."

Interviewer: The last question I wanted to ask you Karen is if you have any notion, any guess, as to where your relationship with Jim would be today if you hadn't had any family visits for the past several years?

Karen: It's hard to say. I wouldn't even want to think of it. It would be really difficult. I don't know how to answer that.

5

Results

The results of this research project were divided into two main sections. The first represents an analysis of the protocol responses (see Appendix B) of both groups of subjects. Part of that analysis is concerned exclusively with the conjugal visiting experience, and especially its sexual aspects, while the larger portion consists of a contrast of the "felt meanings" of the two respective types of visits, i.e., conjugal versus regular. The latter section includes data collected one year after the initial interviews were conducted and is evaluated in the context of whether or not it confirms the two basic hypotheses that were tested in this project.

It should perhaps be mentioned here that the questionnaires ultimately used in this study were not exactly coincident with those initially constructed. Pre-testing with ex-convicts from Delancey Street Foundation, as well as suggestions made by inmates in the first half dozen or so interviews, resulted in modifications of some questions and the deletion of others. However, each man, in each respective group, was, finally, asked a uniform and consistent set of questions.

Certain inherent limitations of this kind of study were mentioned in Chapter 3, but bear further commentary here. The most intensive efforts were made to select two groups of married prisoners who differed critically from each other only with respect to a single variable—whether or not they were receiving conjugal visits. For the most part, the matching process was more successful than had been anticipated. There was a striking correspondence between experimental and comparison groups along the dimensions of ethnicity, mean age, years married, crimes committed, and time served. Still, it is difficult, if not impossible, in a naturalistic study to insure that two selected groups will differ only in terms of a particular "treatment factor" whose value one is interested in measuring. And this was certainly true in the present study, in which the most striking methodological limitation was obtaining inmates, for both groups, with the same custody status.

Had this been successfully accomplished, two significant consequences would have been realized. First, both groups would have been drawn from the same environmental setting in a rather large state prison where the differences between any two sectors can be considerable. Second, there would have been an optimal probability that the behavioral difficulties and internal emotional conflicts of both groups were essentially congruent, since custody status is a function of how a man presents himself behaviorally and of the degree to which he is able to master his impulses.

Unfortunately, neither of these conditions was actually met because it proved impossible to find subjects satisfying the necessary criteria (see Chapter 3). Thus, as the data below are contrasted, it will be useful to bear this limitation in mind. On the other hand, it is vital to note that despite these differing custody classifications, the men in the comparative group shared many relevant similarities with their fellow prisoners in the experimental group.

Comparison of Protocol Responses

Frequency of Visits and Total Number of Visits

It was thought useful to gather data on both the frequency of wives' visits and the total number of visits, but it was realized only after the collection of data was completed that those figures did not yield meaningful results. The reasons for this were twofold. First, regular visits and conjugal visits occur at considerably different time intervals, the former being allowed once weekly while the latter generally occur much less often—once every 30 days to once every two and one half to three months. Additionally, men who receive conjugal visits may receive regular visits as well. Therefore, it was not deemed useful or productive to compare those figures since the absolute numbers, in and of themselves, would not convey anything of significance.

Suitability and Privacy of Visiting Facilities

Prisoners rarely have anything positive to say about the conditions of their captive state. Hence, it was impressive that the overwhelming majority of men receiving conjugal visits regarded the cottage or trailer in which such visits took place as basically suitable, both from the standpoint of physical comfort and in terms of providing a general sense of personal privacy (see Table 5-1).

The reservations most often mentioned by those men who had conjugal visits had to do with some of the trailers needing renovation and better maintenance, though these were minor concerns in general. Regarding the issue of privacy, 11 of the men mentioned an *awareness* of the guntower not too many yards away from the trailer, while two inmates who used the apartment commented on the regular passage of correctional officers on their way to the tennis courts a short distance away. However, overall the men were quite satisfied with the location and quality of the physical space provided for these intimate visits.

On the other hand, the comparative group was more than a little dissatisfied with the suitability of its visiting sites. Fifteen of the men (75 percent) found them lacking in either comfort or privacy or both. That proportion included all of the men in protective custody, who complained about crowded and noisy

Table 5-1
Perceived Suitability of Visiting Facilities
(Responses to Question 4)[a]

Inmate Group	Visiting Facility	Suitable		Unsuitable		Total	
		Number	Percent	Number	Percent	Number	Percent
Experimental	Conjugal	19	95	1	5	20	100
Comparative	Minimum custody	4	20	3	15		
	Close custody	1	5	1	5		
	Protective custody	0		11	55		
		5	25	15	75	20	100

[a]All question numbers refer to Family Visiting Questionnaire (see Appendix B).

conditions, the glass partition and use of phones for communication, and the pain involved in being unable to ever touch their wives. There was also some indication of "paranoid" suspicion concerning the privacy of their phone conversations, although in prison settings nothing is beyond possibility.

Other comments indicative of the kinds of limitations felt by the men who received regular visits (especially in protective custody) included the following:

The glass partition and the use of phones alienate whatever could come of our relationship. It discourages continued visits.

There's no privacy, no contact. It's like a torture chamber. It's better to communicate by letter.

You get the idea you're always being listened to on the phones.

Privacy is a problem. The kids hear people making a lot of comments I'd rather they didn't hear, plus I don't dig people staring at my wife.

The sun glaring on the glass partition doesn't allow me to see my wife for long periods.

My wife feels like she's visiting a "friend" since her only contact with me is by phone.

They strip search us beforehand so why can't they allow us contact visits?

It was clear that inmates who were able to share over 44 hours with their wives, in fairly private circumstances, had considerably fewer complaints about visiting area suitability than did those who saw their wives for only a few hours in a much more constrained environment.

Duration of Visits

All subjects were asked to estimate how long the visits with their wives "seemed," in contrast to their actual duration. The intention was to obtain some index as to perceived versus actual time lapse during visits. It was anticipated that a man's estimate of length of the visit would, in most cases, fall below the actual time interval involved, and this was born out by the results shown in Table 5-2.

The main reason offered for the contracted time estimate from the men with conjugal visits had to do with the fact that while such visits span three different days, they include only one *full* day. Thus, the first and third days are experienced as incomplete, with only the second day being unaffected either by getting the facility fixed up and settling in, or by chores connected to cleaning up and preparing to leave.

For the men who received regular visits, the critical element accounting for the diminished perceived time duration was typically reflected by comments such as: "It speeds up if you're into heavy stuff," and "It seems like about one hour if things are really stimulating." These remarks suggested that conversations highly charged with emotional content contributed to making the visit seem much briefer than it actually was.

Emotional Context of the Visits

The 40 subjects were asked to describe their thoughts and feelings (including fantasies) for the 24 hour period preceding and following each visit with their

Table 5-2
Actual versus Experienced Time of Visits
(Responses to Question 5)

Inmate Group	Type of Visit	Actual Time (Mean)	Experienced Time (Mode)
Experimental (N=20)	Conjugal	44 hours	About 24 hours
Comparative (N=20)	Regular	5 hours	1-3 hours

wives. There was a striking uniformity evident here as reflected in two main clusters: three-fourths of the men in both groups stated that feelings of anxiety or nervousness were most pronounced during the time just prior to the visit; the most dominant feeling experienced after the visit was depression, reported by 70 percent of men who had conjugal visits and 60 percent of those who had received ordinary visits (see Table 5-3).

It is worth noting that three times as many men in the comparative group had problems sleeping just prior to the visits. This may be partly due to the more frustrating circumstances under which regular visits take place, their relative brevity, and the consequent desire to ensure that no portion of that valuable time will be wasted.

Some verbatim statements revealed just how intense are the emotions stimulated by the visits that men received from their wives. Those that follow were concerned with states of being after conjugal visits have come to an end:

> I feel a little lighter, but I find I have to spend some time alone in my bed, and after that only with my closest friend.

> I feel depressed, but I also feel my wife leaves me something to hang onto.

Table 5-3
Feelings Experienced Before and After Visits[a]
(Responses to Question 7)

| State of Being | Before Visits | | After Visits | |
	Experimental (N=20)	Comparative (N=20)	Experimental (N=20)	Comparative (N=20)
Anxious-nervous	15	15	0	1
Depressed	0	0	14	12
Sleep problems	2	6	0	0
Peaceful-relaxed	1	0	4	3
Tired	0	0	1	0
Emotionally drained	0	0	1	1
Happy	0	0	1	1
Angry	0	0	0	1
Hurt	0	0	0	1
Thinking about what we'll say	1	0	0	0

[a]More than one response per subject was possible.

Terribly depressed. I think, "When will this shit ever end?" It takes me over a week to readjust.

It's a bummer. I discipline myself not to think about it.

It's hell. She goes one way and you another.

I miss her a lot, but I feel peaceful.

A somewhat different tone pervades the statements of the prisoners having ordinary visits:

I feel sick to my stomach. The depression lasts several days.

Floating, anxious, a desire to get out, and a fantasy of touching her.

Very quiet and passive, like being in a daze. I just stay in my room and think.

It's a bum trip. You have some warmth and communication and then you come back to this.

Mentally fucked, burnt out, mentally exhausted. I go to sleep afterwards.

Just like a zombie.

It hurts more, you feel like you wanna cry—like you just lost your girl.

While both groups of prisoners experienced the expected reactions to involuntary separation from a loved one, there was a more poignant and bitter tone to the comments made by men in the comparative group. This may be accounted for by assuming that the visits satisfied a narrower range of emotional needs over a shorter period of time so that their depression and anger was less tempered by expressions of attendant satisfactions.

Factors Directly Related to Prisoners' Wives

Practical Difficulties

All subjects were asked whether or not their wives experienced serious physical or financial difficulties in order to visit them. Their responses are summarized in Table 5-4.

The problems mentioned most often had to do with the cost of food for the conjugal visit (averaging about $30-$35); the absence of a car in the family, which meant relying on a friend or a long and arduous bus ride; and, in a few cases, wives having had to drive from as far away as Los Angeles, San Diego, or

Table 5-4
Physical or Financial Problems Attendant to Wives Visits
(Responses to Question 14)

Inmate Group	Problems		No Problems		Total	
	Number	Percent	Number	Percent	Number	Percent
Experimental (N=20)	8	40	12	60	20	100
Comparative (N=20)	14	70	6	30	20	100

Ukiah. In these latter instances, the cost of gas was an additional problem. For those wives who traveled from distant cities the necessity of paying for a motel room on the evening prior to the visit was a further financial burden.

Notwithstanding those difficulties, all of the wives *did* visit, although almost twice as many wives in the comparative group reported such problems as those in the experimental group. It may be that wives in the latter group tend not to mention, dwell upon, or complain about the difficulties inherent in visiting because of the wider scope of their experiences during the course of the visits themselves. It should also be borne in mind that wives who made regular visits made the sacrifices they did in order to *speak* with their husbands for four to six *hours* while their counterparts *lived* with their husbands for two *days*.

Degree of Wife's Comfort in Prison Setting

It was assumed that visiting one's husband on prison grounds may have caused some degree of discomfort for the wives involved. Thus, each subject was asked whether his wife seemed to him comfortable or ill at ease during his visits with her. As indicated in Table 5-5, there was a considerable contrast in experiences for the two sets of wives.

The results here have a broad and direct correlation with the extent to which the various visiting facilities were perceived as being suitable in the first instance (see Table 5-1). If one adjusts for the fact that some wives on conjugal visits became comfortable after their initial visits, then fully 80 percent of such wives can be seen as having felt comfortable during their visits in a cottage or trailer while that was true of only 50 percent of the wives who were making regular visits.

The only two adverse comments made by men in the experimental group were, "She's ill at ease. It's not her own home," and "She's sad because it's unnatural here." On the other hand, the men in the comparative group made

Table 5-5
Wife Perceived as Comfortable During Visits
(Responses to Question 11)

	Comfortable		Uncomfortable		Gradual Adjustment	
Inmate Group	Number	Percent	Number	Percent	Number	Percent
Experimental (N=20)	12	60	4	20	4	20
Comparative (N=20)	10	50	10	50	0	

much stronger statements regarding the distinct discomfort they noticed in their wives. A few sample responses included the following:

> She can't really express herself. The kids climb on the table trying to get through the window to me.

> The partition makes her cry during the visits.

> She says she can't stand the phone and the partition.

> She seems distant. She's Mexican and she can't stand being separated from me.

> She feels ill at ease when someone is behind her and the reflection on the glass prevents her from seeing me.

Frustrations of Prison Life

All subjects were asked whether or not they had discussed the hardships and frustrations of prison life with their wives. The resultant responses were nearly coincident. In the experimental group, 11 men said they had shared such frustrations with their wives while nine did not, while the comparative group was split down the middle. The rationales for both sets of decisions were surprisingly similar. Those who did speak of the difficulties of incarceration tended to be somewhat younger and welcomed the support, sympathy, understanding, and encouragement that such openness frequently elicited. On the other hand, there were those men who had considerable pride in their powers of endurance whose most common explanation for their silence on these matters was some variation of "She has enough to worry about without my adding to it." Thus there were no significant intergroup differences, although there did appear to be a clear-cut division between two different types of men in both groups: (1) those who desired an empathic understanding of their condition, and (2) those who

valued controlled understatement of the constant pressures and deprivations that
they were forced to live with.

The Question of Extramarital Affairs

All married prisoners, especially those serving long sentences, realize the tempta-
tions, conflicts, and anguish that their wives are subjected to as their terms stretch
from months to years. Thus it was deemed important to determine how prisoners
dealt with the issue of the possible involvement of their wives in extramarital relationships. It seemed useful to phrase this question so that it was direct without
seeming provocative or spurred by motives of prurient interest. Hence the
question posed to each inmate was, "Have you ever asked your wife whether or
not she has had any extramarital affairs while you've been in prison?" This
inquiry could be answered with a simple yes or no, or with further elaboration.
It was then decided, on the basis of the emotional tone of a man's response,
whether it seemed appropriate to further ask, "If so, what was her response, or
if not, why not?" Though this method of interviewing prevented a strict
uniformity in the pattern of responses, it maximized the possibility of obtaining
valuable information without insulting the subjects or violating their sense of
privacy.

It should be noted that while the experimental group consisted of 20 men
who were receiving conjugal visits *presently*, most of them had previously served
time when such visits were not available. This means that the majority of the
wives of these men had spent at least some period of time in the same situation
that the wives of the men in the comparative group presently found themselves
in.

Table 5-6 compares the responses of the two groups of subjects with regard
to this delicate issue. The figures suggest little difference between the two groups
with respect to the proportion of men who directly confronted their wives about
whether they had had extramarital affairs during the husband's imprisonment
(30 percent in one case and 40 percent in the other). But two factors of a more
subtle nature require comment. The first is that a quarter of the men in the
experimental group said that any affairs that their wives had mentioned having
in the past had stopped completely as soon as they began to participate in
conjugal visits.

The second factor emerged when the answers to this question were separated
into three quite distinct categories that might be labeled "I believe she's loyal,"
"I don't want to know," and "It's understandable." The experimental group
produced an extremely high proportion of responses of the third type and a
relatively higher proportion of the second type (that is, the desire to remain
ignorant). The comparative group was essentially divided evenly between belief

Table 5-6
Number of Wives Asked About Extramarital Affairs
(Responses to Question 19)

	Yes		No		Total	
Inmate Group	Number	Percent	Number	Percent	Number	Percent
Experimental (N=20)	8	40	12	60	20	100
Comparative (N=20)	6	30	14	70	20	100

in the wives' loyalty and a desire not to know, with only two responses indicating that it's an understandable state of affairs.

Typical responses of the three respective types described above are offered below:

1. *Loyal*

   She's above it.

   I believe she's loyal.

   It's OK with me, but she's not interested.

   I believe she's faithful.

   I really don't think she is.

2. *Don't Want to Know*

   What I don't know doesn't bother me.

   I said to her, "Don't tell me about it and don't get pregnant."

   I told her, "Don't tell me or there's trouble."

3. *Understandable*

   She has, and she probably will again, but I don't expect it will affect our marriage adversely.

   It's understandable since I'm unavailable, but it's a purely sexual thing.

   She said she did. I know that if I show jealousy I lose her. It has no negative effect on our marriage.

   I would hope that she had, especially early on.

   I urge her to if she's frustrated.

A few observations are in order regarding these remarks. First, there seemed to be a considerably greater need in the comparative group to believe that one's wife was absolutely faithful, historical evidence and human nature notwithstanding. It may be that the men in the experimental group did not use this kind of rigid denial as much because they were then having sexual relations with their wives and may have been able to perceive, more flexibly, certain basic truths about the likely results of prolonged deprivation.

Second, there was a distinct absence in almost all those comments in which extramarital sex was acknowledged of any flavor of the traditional middle class hypocrisy regarding "unfaithfulness." Instead, a direct and simple appreciation was expressed for what is, after all, a deep instinctual need, combined with a sincere belief that a wife's fulfillment of that need does not *necessarily* imply irreparable damage to the marital relationship.

Family-related Factors

The Prisoners' Children

Since just about half of both groups of subjects had children, all subjects were asked if their wives usually brought the children with them when they visited (see Table 5-7). In addition, for those children of inmates who did visit, the men were asked what comments, if any, they would make regarding their fathers' imprisonment (see Table 5-8).

It is clear from the results that virtually all prisoners and their wives considered it valuable that their children were included in visits, despite the social stigma and possible emotional upheaval the children may have experienced. The one exception was a man receiving conjugal visits whose seven children range in age from 16 to 25. In that instance both parents felt that, because of the children's ages, it was more appropriate that they come during regular visiting

Table 5-7
Number of Children Brought by Wives to Visits
(Responses to Question 8)

	Yes		No		Not Applicable		Total	
Inmate Group	Number	Percent	Number	Percent	Number	Percent	Number	Percent
Experimental (N=20)	10	50	1	5	9	45	20	100
Comparative (N=20)	11	55	0		9	45	20	100

Table 5-8
Children's Comments Regarding Fathers' Imprisonment
(Responses to Question 9)

Comment	Experimental Group (N=10)		Comparative Group (N=11)	
	Number	Percent	Number	Percent
When are you coming home?	4	40	5	46
No comment	5	50	1	9
Too young to speak	0		2	18
They cry	0		2	18
Ask about men in towers	0		1	9
Mention remarks by classmates	1	10	0	

times so that husband and wife might have the conjugal visits in total privacy. The fact that all but one man in the experimental group asked their wives to bring their children (in most cases always, in a few cases sometimes) suggested the importance attached to the visit as an opportunity for the entire family to be together as a unit, rather than a simple desire to utilize the visit for purposes of emotional and sexual intimacy with one's wife.

It is clear from Table 5-8 that the most frequent comment made by the children of prisoners, in both groups, had to do with when their fathers will be with them again. The pathos of that question lies in the fact that, most often, because of the indeterminate sentence (currently in the process of being modified) a man is unable to give his child any answer at all.

Some of the things the children *did* say reflected the extent of the distress and confusion they experienced as a result of extended separations from their fathers. One three and one half year old girl had this exchange with her father: "Do you love my mommy?" "Yes, why do you ask?" "Because you're not home with us."

Interestingly, 50 percent of the children of men in the experimental group made no comment regarding their fathers being in prison while this was true of only one child in the comparative group. This may be at least partially explained by the possibility that the former group of children had better opportunity to see their father's situation as one of relative normality. Spending two days with them in a private cottage or trailer, although geographically separated from where they lived, at least approximated a home environment. This was decidedly not the case for the other children, who visit their fathers in very different settings as described in Chapter 4. This line of speculation is further buttressed by the fact that several of the men in the experimental group stated that their younger children "think I'm in an out of town school," or "working here," or "believe I'm in the military." Because of the age and sensitivity of these children, their fathers have said nothing to alter their beliefs.

Two children from the experimental group were described as being particularly quiet and withdrawn about their feelings concerning their father's imprisonment. Both were boys who had witnessed their father's arrests at the family home, one at the age of four and the other at five and one half. The latter child was so shaken and confused by the experience that he has been seeing a psychiatrist regularly for the past two years.

The children of those men who received regular visits were frequently described as depressed and bitter, a fact not specifically included in Table 5-8. That was not the case with children in the experimental group. Much of this difference is probably traceable to the contrasting environments in which these respective visits occurred. Two of the regular visit children were described as crying frequently during the visits and not saying very much. Others complained about being controlled by the guards with respect to how much they could hug, kiss, and in general express affection to their fathers, a problem the children in the conjugal visit group never confront in the confines of the trailers or cottages, or indeed in the outdoor yard behind the cottages.

One young prisoner made this comment regarding his seven year old son: "He heard I was part of a gang so he started one at school. He says he wants to stay here with me, and be like me. He saw me arrested on the front lawn and cursed officers, saying, 'They're keeping you away from me. I hate them!' "

All in all, no child who visits his father in prison can find it an altogether pleasant experience, although the simulation of a warm home setting can do much to make such visits more valuable and less frustrating than those that take place in crowded visiting rooms under often strained circumstances.

What Do They Talk About?

An effort to determine what prisoners and their wives discussed most revealed some striking similarities and a few possibly significant differences as shown in Table 5-9.

It is apparent that concerns about the future—hopes, dreams, aspirations, projects (real or otherwise)—represented the primary topic of conversation among prisoners and their wives in both groups. And, given what has been said about the passage of time in prison (see Chapter 2), this is not at all surprising. Time stands still in prison. The past becomes a blurred memory, while the future looms as a forever unrealized dream potential. Thus, 95 percent of the men in the experimental group and 85 percent of those in the comparative group selected this item as the one most discussed with their wives.

Other findings that stood out were that a larger proportion of men in the comparative group spent time on money concerns and issues regarding their children. That this may have been due, in part, to the lack of extended emotional contact afforded these men may be a possible explanation. Inmates who received conjugal visits had a greater opportunity to see how their kids were doing by

Table 5-9
Family Matters Discussed Most With Wife[a]
(Responses to Question 13)

Inmate Group	Future Plans		Marital Relationship		Children		Money		Other	
	Number	Percent	Number	Percent	Number	Percent	Number	Percent	Number	Percent
Experimental (N=20)	19	95	4	20	2	10	2	10	1	5
Comparative (N=20)	17	85	3	15	6	30	7	35	3	15

[a]More than one response per subject was possible.

communicating with them over a 44 hour period. One might also imagine that the deep satisfactions of spending leisure time with one's family would tend to reduce interest in purely monetary issues.

Benefits of Visits

Each man was asked what was the most important benefit of the visits he received from his wife (and children, where applicable). There were subtle distinctions between the two groups which were more obvious in the men's comments than in the figures recorded in Table 5-10. One had to do with the much larger number of men in the experimental group who viewed the most valuable benefits of their visits as the stabilization and enhancement of the marital and family relationship. This was true of 75 percent of those men as opposed to only 30 percent of the men in the comparative group (see sum of first three items in Table 5-10). Of the men who received regular visits, nine mentioned just the opportunity to see and talk with their wives as of primary value, while three saw the visits as proof their spouses still loved them. None of the men in the experimental group mentioned either of these factors, and perhaps for obvious reasons since they are offered the possibility of doing more than merely *seeing* and *speaking* with their wives.

Still, there are particular nuances that emerge only in the context of the men's actual statements. Those men who received conjugal visits emphasize such things

Table 5-10
Major Perceived Benefit of Visits
(Responses to Question 23)

Perceived benefit	Experimental Group (N=20)		Comparative Group (N=20)	
	Number	*Percent*	*Number*	*Percent*
Keeps marriage together	7	35	3	15
Fosters emotional closeness and mutual understanding	4	20	1	5
Just being with my family	4	20	2	10
Relieves tension of prison environment	5	25	2	10
Just seeing and talking to her	0		9	45
Proves she still loves me	0	__	3	15
Total	20	100	20	100

as intimacy, increased understanding, emotional closeness, etc. as vital mainsprings of the visit. Comments such as the following were illustrative of that perspective:

> To fulfill my obligations as a husband and parent and to provide a type of emotional support to enable my wife to sustain the role of both parents.

> I don't have to go back to society as a complete blank, because I've achieved a better understanding of myself through my wife.

> Feeling that my marriage is stable and enduring.

> Getting lots of moral support from my wife.

> Peace of mind.

> Living like a human being for a while.

> Being able to create the type of environment that is pleasing to both of us.

The statements noted above suggest a combination of self-reflection, an increased sense of dignity, and hope for the future as central elements of the conjugal visits' meaning for many of these men. By contrast, these remarks were made by subjects in the comparative group:

> It's better than nothing, but it's torture.

> It's a release valve.

> Just seeing her.

> Knowing someone cares about you.

> Just being able to talk with her.

There was a much greater appreciation here for the visit as a present-oriented event providing some relief from the vicissitudes of institutional life through contact with a loved one. But there was a noticeable absence of any suggestion of a developing, explorative, or dynamic relationship compared to the couples in the experimental group. This may be largely attributed to the very restricted conditions under which these visits took place since even with the best of intentions, intimacy, self-appraisal, and planning for the future were all but impossible. Only one man mentioned the opportunity for sexual intercourse as the primary benefit of conjugal visits, and even this response came in the context of his belief that it helped to maintain a close emotional tie with his wife.

Perceived Purpose of the Conjugal Visits

The last question posed to the men in both groups concerned their beliefs concerning the "real" intentions of the CDC in initiating a family visiting program. Perhaps it should be pointed out once more that most of the prisoners viewed "family visits" as synonymous with "conjugal visits" and it was with that assumption that they responded to the question. A summary of their stated opinions of this matter appear in Table 5-11.

Perhaps the most outstanding result was the almost unanimous (35 of 40 subjects) belief that the visits serve as an instrument of control even if they were not initiated with that purpose in mind. Statements like the following illustrated that sentiment:

You don't get up in the man's face when you got conjugal visits.

It [the visits] keeps the lid on.

They keep the inmates in line.

It cuts down on violence because the most important thing to a man is a woman.

It curbs frustration and violence.

They keep the heat off the staff.

While it's true that a man's visits are not denied him because of minor infractions, they can be and are denied for whatever is considered a "major" disciplinary violation. Since many, if not most, of these are connected with violent behavior or the smuggling of contraband, the incidence of such behavior tends to be sharply reduced among the men who receive conjugal visits. How the visits may be utilized as a peculiar form of administrative control will be more closely examined in the next chapter.

Table 5-11
Perceived Purpose of CDC in Permitting Conjugal Visits[a]
(Responses to Question 22)

Inmate Group	Stabilize Marriage		Decrease Homosexuality		Instrument of Control	
	Number	Percent	Number	Percent	Number	Percent
Experimental (N=20)	15	75	6	30	18	90
Comparative (N=20)	12	60	11	55	17	85

[a]More than one response was possible per subject.

Two other results were notable. One was the fairly large proportion of men who believed that, in addition to the by-product of social control, the corrections department was interested in helping to stabilize the marital relationships. The other was the considerably higher proportion (almost twice as many) of men in the comparative group who believed that one of the purposes of instituting conjugal visits was to reduce homosexuality. It is possible that this differential response was related to homosexuality being a more widespread phenomenon among those men who never have an opportunity for heterosexual contact. The men in the conjugal visiting group confirmed this possibility by informally remarking that they did not perceive nor were they aware of nearly as much homosexuality among men in their custody area of the prison as in those areas where conjugal visits were nonexistent or extremely infrequent.

Data Collected from Conjugal Visit Group Only

The intention in the preceding section was to compare the nature and value of two very different kinds of visits for men in prison. This section is devoted exclusively to the presentation of data gathered only from men in the group receiving conjugal visits. It was hoped that an analysis of these data would provide a broader and fuller picture of the meaning of such visits in the context of the total prison experience.

Almost half of the questions asked of men in this group were related in one way or another to the issue of sexuality. Though this investigator was concerned that the delicacy of such inquiries might result in some men taking offense at being asked for details of considerable intimacy, this was never the case. In fact, on several occasions the men offered more information than was requested. One can only speculate about why this was so. Some of it seemed to be the result of the generally good rapport established with the inmates, although two other factors also suggested themselves. Prisoners as a group seem to be less hypocritical, even if more impulsive, about their sexuality than are most middle class persons. In addition, the prisoners clearly considered the family visiting program extremely valuable and may have believed that open and honest responses to questions about sex might have increased the likelihood of that program being expanded by prison officials and given greater priority in the total schema of "rehabilitation."

Time, Food, and Cleanliness

Three elements that structure the conjugal visit in ways that at first glance seem superficial are time, food, and the physical condition of the facility used. These elements seem trivial, perhaps, because we take them for granted in everyday life.

Most of us, after all, can eat the foods we wish to, arrange our homes to suit us, and alter the subjective experience of time by choosing to engage in activities that will hasten or slow its passage. But none of these are automatically within the control of the average prisoner at Soledad except during conjugal visits. Hence, it was deemed worthwhile to inquire about some limited aspects of each of these topics.

Each man was asked whether or not prisoners who used the cottages or trailers left them neat and clean for the next man, namely themselves. About two-thirds (13) stated that they did while seven said they did not. Of the seven, several had mixed comments of the "some do and some don't" variety. One, more vocal than the rest, stated that his "wife spends a couple of hours cleaning the place up," while another reported that "They leave it dirty—the stove, the refrigerator, and, you know, the rooms need sweeping and mopping, which my wife and I wind up doing."

In general, then, the inmates seemed to have enough consideration for their fellow prisoners to spend an hour or two cleaning up for the next family. The exceptions may be accounted for either by a general indifference, or by the depression that begins to develop toward the end of the visit, and that may inhibit a systematic cleanup. In any event, only one or two of the complaints suggested that the men had a total disregard for the physical condition of the facility and how the next man would find it.

All subjects in this group were asked whether or not their wives brought any special foods that are either not included in the standard prison fare or are available rarely. The vast majority, 80 percent, answered affirmatively while only four responded negatively. The latter group explained the absence of favorite foods brought by their wives as a direct result of economic limitations. The list of items brought by wives in somewhat better financial circumstances included sweets, fish, barbecued chicken, casseroles, Cheerios, steak, spaghetti, health foods, tacos, burritos, chocolate cake, fried chicken, crabs, oysters, avocados, artichokes, Chateaubriand, and milk. Steak was mentioned most often (by seven men) and with greatest enthusiasm.

What was most striking was the lack of congruence between the rather considerably efforts on the part of the wives to bring all sorts of gourmet delights and the reaction of the men to them. All the men indicated that they were, of course, deeply appreciative of being able to have these things, but they simultaneously commented that they were not really very significant, not as important, for example, as their wives bringing special clothes that they were permitted to wear for the duration of the visit. This suggested that the opportunity to differentiate oneself, to "costume oneself," so to speak, with some uniqueness in terms of style, flair, color, and fit, was of much greater value than dining on the food of free men. This was especially interesting in demonstrating just how homogeneous and oppressively similar prisoners are forced to look in the penitentiary. Rarely are inmates allowed to set themselves off from the mob by means of their clothing, personal adornments, the way they wear their hair, or by growing a beard. Clearly, how a man may "present" himself seems to be valued more by him than whether or not he has steak for dinner.

Naturally all of the men interviewed would have liked the conjugal visits to be more frequent and to last longer. Still, when asked what they believed was an ideal time frame for such visits, given the limitations of facilities and the number of men eligible for such visits, their responses seemed eminently reasonable, and are summarized in Table 5-12.

These results appear to counter the notion, popular among large segments of our citizenry, that prisoners "want everything." In fact, only one man indicated a desire for the visits to last a period of time that might be viewed as unrealistic or excessive. The four who said it was sufficient as it was amplified their responses by pointing out that any increased length of time would probably lead to a corresponding increase of pain and depression at the point of eventual separation.

What was especially noteworthy here was the high proportion of inmates who considered that the mere addition of 24 hours or so would make for an ideal visit if it were structured so as to include three complete days. The most frequent complaint about the present visits was that although they spanned three *different* days, they included only one *entire* day (the visits began at 2:00 P.M. and ended at 10:00 A.M.).

The Issue of Sex

Obviously, the opportunity to continue a sexual relationship with one's wife is of paramount importance to the men who enjoy conjugal visits. But that satisfaction is embedded in a larger and more complex psychological framework. To understand more fully how sexual intimacy between a man and his wife is affected by its taking place on the grounds of a state prison, the men were asked questions regarding its overall significance, the relative responsiveness of their

Table 5-12
Prisoners' Views of Ideal Time Period for Conjugal Visits
(Responses to Question 6)

Ideal Time	Frequency	Percent
72 hours (3 full days)	13	65
Sufficient as is	4	20
Two full days	1	5
One week	1	5
Just longer than it is	1	5

wives, their own degree of experienced pleasure, and about any anxiety related to the infrequency of such sexual opportunities. Their responses are shown in Table 5-13.

The question about the relative value of sex was asked as follows: "Sex is obviously a very important factor in family visits. Is there anything that is even more important to you during these visits?" It soon became clear that this was an unfortunate way to phrase the inquiry, since most of the men stated that a more appropriate and relevant question was, "Is there anything *as* important as sex? . . . ", and it was to this reformulated question that the men addressed their responses.

The overwhelming majority felt that indeed other factors were as crucial to them as sexual contact. Most frequently mentioned was "emotional closeness" or some variant thereof (11 men), and "a better understanding of each other" (three men). One man responded, "The woman's touch," while another said, "Everyone wants to feel close to home." These remarks certainly did not minimize the extreme premium placed by the men on physical intimacy, but they did provide a sense of how prominent their more diffuse longings are—the desire to satisfy dependency needs, affirm self-worth, experience being "well-understood," feel "at home," etc. These feelings were subtle, but repeatedly struck this investigator as having at least as much personal value to the inmates as the opportunity for satisfying basic sexual needs.

It was thought that the relatively long time periods between visits might cause some sexual anxiety and consequent dysfunction among the men once they were with their wives. A little less than a third of the group acknowledged that this was so, although most stressed that that was the case particularly during the first two or three visits (which were often preceded by months or years of not having had sexual contact with their spouses). Premature ejaculation was the most common form in which this anxiety expressed itself, although one man experienced ejaculatory incompetence. It may also be assumed that some fraction of those subjects who responded negatively to this question may also have experienced some problems of adjustment, but might have been reluctant to express it for reasons having to do with their self-image.

There was some interest in determining what effect a prison environment had on a man's enjoyment of sex with his wife. The findings here were somewhat surprising. Four said there was no difference, that although they *valued* it more, they experienced about the same degree of satisfaction or pleasure. But, half of the men said they enjoyed it more, many because of its irregularity. Others had more specific comments, like the following, to account for their increased perception of pleasure:

We play a game of seeing who can hold out longest before giving in. We don't rush it.

My wife dresses more sexy and prepares herself more carefully than at home.

Table 5-13
Experiences Related to Sexual Relations During Conjugal Visits
(Responses to Questions 15-18)

Anything as important as sex during visit?		Experience anxiety about sexual "performance?"		Enjoyment of sex during visit versus at home			Wife as sexually responsive at home?	
Yes	No	Yes	No	More	Less	Same	Yes	No
17 (85%)	3 (15%)	6 (30%)	14 (70%)	10 (50%)	6 (30%)	4 (20%)	15 (75%)	5 (25%)
Total: 20 (100%)		Total: 20 (100%)		Total: 20 (100%)			Total: 20 (100%)	

More because of the long period of time without any sex.

Sex is more satisfying now, but many other factors have developed in our relationship during the course of the conjugal visits.

There were six men who stated that they enjoyed sex less during the conjugal visits than at home. One mentioned the inhibiting effect of his ten year old son; another said "It ain't like being in your own home." A third talked about the tension generated by trying to "push the frequency of sex" throughout the visit. Yet another said, "I concentrate on *her* satisfaction."

The men's perception of their wives' general responsiveness in prison, as compared to at home, suffered from the limited reliability of one person judging the complex physical and emotional behavior of another, despite the closeness of the two people to each other. Still, since it was not possible (nor in this investigator's opinion appropriate) to interview the wives, this secondary source of information was presumed to have at least some value. Three-fourths of the men reported that their wives seemed just as comfortable having sex during the visits as in their home environment. This finding is somewhat counterintuitive, as it might be anticipated that most women would not experience a prison as a place that facilitates the kind of relaxation associated with optimal sexual responsiveness. On the other hand, these were, after all, the husbands' impressions, and may not accord with the actual experiences of their wives, who may have concealed their uneasiness and faked the degree of their sexual pleasure in order to enhance their husbands' satisfaction and sense of "manliness."

The supposition above is lent some support by comments like these: "More so, because she's trying harder to satisfy me," and "Probably more because of the specialness of the whole thing." Here it would seem as if some of the men may have been mistakenly interpreting efforts by their wives to maximize the pleasure of sex as an index of how the women themselves were feeling—an interpretation open to question. Still, one would be wise not to discount this information without contradictory comments from the wives themselves.

What About the Unmarried Prisoner?

Conjugal visits are presently permitted in California's prisons only for legally married inmates. It did not seem useful to solicit the opinions of subjects in the comparative group as to whether they considered such a policy discriminatory, since their collective responses appeared self-evident. But it was thought more valuable to ask the same question of the married men since their attitudes did not have the same degree of personal investment. Thus, all of the men who received such visits were asked first if they considered the exclusion of single men to be discriminatory, and second whether or not they felt common-law wives or girlfriends ought to be allowed the same privilege as their own wives.

The response was almost unanimous: 19 of the 20 men stated that the program as it now exists is indeed discriminatory, and the same number favored such visits being opened up to both common-law wives and girlfriends. The sole exception was an inmate whose only reason for disagreeing with the others was expressed as follows: "One guy could mess up the program. The CDC might consider that the program was being abused, and cut the whole thing out." Obviously, his concerns were pragmatic rather than moralistic. Some of the implications of this strong support for expanding the criteria of eligibility for conjugal visits will be elaborated on in the next chapter.

Prisoner Evaluations of the Conjugal Visits

Inmates who received conjugal visits were asked how valuable they were in comparison to any other program available to them in the prison. The result here was unequivocal; there was not a single man who considered any program or service in the institution to be as personally beneficial to him as the conjugal visits. In fact, not a few of the men stared quizzically at the investigator and asked, "What other programs?" They were quick to point out that the only other programs of any substance that existed at all were the marginal ones of vocational training in useless, outmoded trades, and a high school equivalency class. A handful of men mentioned Associate Superintendent E. A. Peterson's community awareness group as worthwhile, but not at all on the same level of importance as the conjugal visits.

What was especially intriguing was the fact that the family visiting program in general, and more specifically conjugal visits, clearly held a unique position in the matrix of prison life. It would be no exaggeration to suggest that it is the only activity within prison walls endorsed by both administration and inmates. That, alone, makes it a phenomenon worth taking a closer look at.

One Year Followup Study

One year after the initial interviews with the 40 original subjects, a followup study was conducted. Its intent was to obtain data that would provide a basis for evaluating the two major hypotheses of this dissertation: (1) that conjugal visits in prison affect parole outcome favorably, and (2) that conjugal visits in prison positively influence subsequent marital stability.

It was anticipated that the followup study would entail a rather straightforward procedure despite the fact that some subjects would by then have been released to their respective residences throughout the state while others would still be incarcerated at Soledad. The investigator maintained a naive expectation that all that was required was to identify and contact the parole agents of the subjects who were no longer in prison and request that they complete the necessary data forms in concert with their respective parolees. The balance of the subjects could be reinterviewed at the correctional facility. For the latter group, institutional disciplinary infractions would be used as a correlative to parole difficulties (see Appendix C, Forms 1-3).

This assumption of a clean and methodical data collection was shattered almost immediately. What did materialize was a sharply telescoped and frustrating education regarding the multiple and often unforeseeable hazards of research in correctional settings. While the detailed vicissitudes of that effort are too convoluted to chronicle fully, it does seem worthwhile to summarize its essential contours.

Contact with officials at Soledad revealed that of the 40 original subjects, 29 had been released since being interviewed a year previously. For this latter group, only the addresses and phone numbers of their parole offices were available. Written communication with these agencies proved largely futile; most requests for information were ignored. Phone calls were more successful, resulting in at least identifying the appropriate parole officer, although about half of the parolees had moved to another part of the state or had been sent to a work furlough program in another area. Finally, after several weeks of Holmesian investigative efforts, all but two of those 29 subjects were located (one by now as far away as Maine). Of the two exceptions, one had died of natural causes in prison and one had been deported to Mexico upon being released. The former had been a member of the comparative group, and the latter of the experimental group.

Thus, it was at least theoretically possible at that point to obtain information on 38 men. However, a handful of parole agents failed to return the data forms, and of the 27 parolees who had been sent the marital status forms by their parole agents, seven failed to respond. This necessitated further phone calls, and in some instances required obtaining marital information from a subject's parole agent instead of from the subject himself. Despite the obstacles catalogued above, comprehensive information on all 38 men was ultimately obtained.

The followup interviews with the 11 men still imprisoned revealed that four of them had begun receiving conjugal visits within five to eight weeks after the investigator had originally interviewed them a year previously. A decision then had to be made as to whether or not to consider them as appropriate subjects for the comparative group. It seemed only reasonable, since they had, in fact, received conjugal visits for about 90 percent of the prior 12 month period (though not at the time they were first selected as part of the comparative sample), to transfer them to the experimental group for purposes of analyzing the results. Thus, with that change and the loss of the two subjects noted above, the experimental group then contained 23 men and the comparative group 15 men.

Testing the Two Hypotheses

Visits and Parole Adjustment. The data regarding the outcomes of the two groups of subjects are summarized in Table 5-14. The operational definitions of "minor" and "serious" parole difficulties may be found in Form 1, Appendix C.

The numerical results in Table 5-14 strongly suggest acceptance of the hypothesis that conjugal visits in prison increase the likelihood of a positive parole outcome. Almost twice the proportion of men in the comparative group (40 percent) experienced some level of parole difficulty (minor or serious) as contrasted with the men in the experimental group (22 percent). The figures for minor parole problems, when considered separately, are even more impressive: the comparative group had five times the fraction of its members in that category as did the experimental group—20 percent versus 4 percent!

It is significant to note that of the four men in the experimental group whose parole problems were serious, all but one were related to heroin addiction, while the remaining one involved an assault on the subject's wife. The one "minor" difficulty was a drunken driving arrest which did not result in a conviction. All but the last mentioned of these men are back in prison as a consequence of new felony convictions or are in jail awaiting trial. In the comparative group the adjustment problems ran a larger gamut, including two auto thefts, one escape from parole supervision, intermittent heroin use, assault of a spouse, and a kidnap and robbery charge. Three of these men have been returned to prison.

A most salient fact about the five experimental group recidivists, besides their high incidence of heroin addiction, was that they had been married just about half as long as the average man in their sample (a mean of 4.7 years as opposed to 9.1 years). Hence, while there appears to be a strong correlation between receiving conjugal visits and successful parole outcome, that correlation would seem to exclude those men who had been married less than five years and were plagued by narcotic addiction as well. At the very least there seems good reason to believe that criminal recidivism for married prisoners may be markedly reduced by the experience of frequent conjugal visits throughout their sentences.

Table 5-14
Relationship of Type of Visit to Parole Outcome

Inmate Group	No Parole Difficulties		Minor Parole Difficulties		Serious Parole Difficulties		Total	
	Number	Percent	Number	Percent	Number	Percent	Number	Percent
Experimental (N=23)	18	79	1	4	4	17	23	100
Comparative (N=15)	9	60	3	20	3	20	15	100

Visits and Marital Stability. The data comparing the marital status of the two groups of subjects are summarized in Table 5-15. Clarification of the meaning of the terms used to categorize relative stability of marriages is provided in Form 2, Appendix C. To summarize, "minimal" or "moderate" problems were considered as those that exist in almost any marital relationship, or those which are being handled to the couples' satisfaction, respectively. "Serious problems" were those in which the couple were experiencing conflicts causing severe stress to the continued existence of the marriage, including the likelihood of an impending separation and/or divorce.

The results presented in Table 5-15 appear to *strongly* confirm the second hypothesis, i.e., the existence of a direct relationship between receiving conjugal visits and subsequent marital stability. The combined rate of separation and divorce in the comparative group (47 percent) was almost four times as high as that in the experimental group (13 percent)! If one considers a marriage with "minimal" or "moderate" problems as relatively satisfactory, then more than double the proportion of men in the experimental group had marriages of that kind, as contrasted with the men in the comparative group.

A further key contrast was made between the total proportion of subjects in the two groups whose marriages were in a state of serious disruption or had already been dissolved (i.e., serious marital problems or separated or divorced). In that instance the results were 22 percent for the experimental group, and 67 percent for the comparative group. What these data mean is that just about three times as many marriages were floundering or had already ended among men not permitted conjugal visits, as opposed to those marriages in which such visits had been regularly available on a monthly basis.

A compelling impressionistic supplement to the results cited above may be found in a sample of comments included by the experimental subjects or their parole agents in their completed data forms. Though not necessarily representative of the complete sample, they did suggest postimprisonment outcomes that are atypical and seem clearly linked to the psychosexual support provided by regular conjugal visits. These excerpts represent just about one-fourth of the experimental subjects:

We have no serious problems. Family visiting helped considerably.

Since my release my wife had another daughter which has bound us even closer. I might add that she was conceived on a family visit, and that it was planned. I have been out almost a year now and hold the same job. . . . In all the successful achievements I have, my wife played a major role—again placing one more advantage to the CDC and the family visiting program.

My relationship with my wife has been harmonious and peaceful. I feel grown up and responsible toward our relationship. Beyond that we need no more, other than the need for each other.

We are more in love than ever and even though things haven't been what I

Table 5-15
Relationship of Type of Visit to Marital Status

Inmate Group	Married: Minimal or Moderate Problems		Married: Serious Problems		Separated		Divorced		Total	
	Number	Percent	Number	Percent	Number	Percent	Number	Percent	Number	Percent
Experimental (N=23)	18	78	2	9	1	4	2	9	23	100
Comparative (N=15)	5	33 1/3	3	20	2	13 1/3	5	33 1/3	15	100

had hoped for [financially] we are well and happy. . . . My wife was able to get pregnant during our very last family visit. Formulating plans for our child has further tightened our relationship and we are both happy beyond words.

[from parole agent] He is residing with his wife and son on an estate where he works part time in exchange for rent. In addition he is attending UCSB where he is carrying 12 units. Last term he received all "A" grades. There has been no indication of parole violation and he has led an exemplary life since being paroled. He seems determined to be a good citizen.

[from parole agent] He has maintained full time employment and is now the director of the Opportunities Industrialization Center in Stockton. He has also accompanied me to elementary schools to give talks on the parole system.

There are no analogous comments regarding men in the comparative group except for one inmate who has become a Jehovah's Witness and attributes his relatively successful marital adjustment to the deep religious faith he and his wife share.

6

Discussion

From the hour of my first imprisonment in a filthy county jail, I recognized the fact that the prison was essentially an institution for the punishment of the poor, and this is one of many reasons why I abhor the prison, and why I recognize it to be my duty to do all in my power to humanize it as far as possible while it exists.

—Eugene V. Debs (1927)

That almost all offenders have significant family ties, for good or ill, is the best kept secret in American corrections.

—Chaiklin (1972)

. . . words like "do-gooder" and "tender-minded" often served to express and perpetuate the disparagement felt for those who were mainly interested in what psychology could do to help people and improve the human condition.

—Tyler (1973)

What Do the Results Mean?

It is believed that the findings of this research project may have major implications that extend from the psychology of imprisonment and related sociological questions to the bedrock assumptions of our entire criminal justice system. Though most inmates and many penal administrators know and will acknowledge that what prisons really do is to isolate from society and punish criminal offenders, the myth of correctional rehabilitation continues as a convenient balm for the American public. But there are voices now being raised to challenge the self-gratifying assumptions of those who are seduced by the mask of altruism flaunted in even our most despicable dungeons.

Silber (1974), in assessing the role of mental health workers in penitentiaries, noted that "Treatment programs are widely carried out without theoretical rationale, or solid empirical support. Little is known concerning the relative efficacy of various treatment programs, if indeed they even work" (p. 240).

Some clinicians have gone so far as to recommend replacing (or at least supplementing) conventional treatment programs in prison by enlisting family involvement and support as a more realistic way of promoting change in criminal behavior. Chaiklin's (1972) comment in this regard is typical: "People do not change in limbo. . . . No correctional program can succeed if it does not include those who the offender will live with after prison. . . " (p. 786).

Even so, certain questions immediately suggest themselves: Don't all prisons have provisions for visiting? Is it not the case that family members are allowed, even encouraged, to visit regularly? Aren't visits the one experience in prison that men uniformly look to with hope and excitement? At first glance it would seem as if the answer to each of those queries is an unequivocal "yes." But that, unfortunately, is not the case. Visiting facilities do exist, in the same way that food, clothing, toilets, and showers exist in prison. Their quality, however, is altogether another matter. Brodsky (1975), who did an intensive study of visits in prison, remarked that "Visiting hours have been set for the convenience of the correctional personnel and the sites of visits have been large, cavernous rooms more suited to drill team exercises and cheerleading than personal discussions" (p. 5).

Thus, while visiting exists, its meaningfulness, its potential as a source for healthy socialization, is sabotaged by the far from ideal circumstances in which it usually takes place. No better description of the frustrations of visiting in such surroundings exists than this one by Levy and Miller (1971), who were themselves confined in a federal prison for a time:[a]

The visiting situation does not provide the possibility for meaningful communication: it is not meant to. . . whether at the farm camp or in the penitentiary, the visiting room is crowded with adults and children. Husband and wife grow apart because they are undergoing profound changes—especially if they are young—and *they neither have the time nor the right atmosphere to communicate what is happening inside one another.* The same is true for children, although the level of communication is very different. Two or three years of a child's life are enormously important in terms of personality development: there is no way in the world a father in prison can relate to that growing child's emotional and physical needs. The only consolation that current visiting practices in Federal prisons bring is the opportunity for the inmate and his family to renew their faith in the existence of one another. . . . Something that we witnessed in the visiting room time and again illustrates the point. After being together for an hour or so, an inmate and his wife may spend the rest of the time staring off into space. They don't have anything more to say. In fact, they have everything to say—except that they can't bring themselves to say it. . . . Conversely, some inmates will talk continuously about anything under the sun in order to cover up their inability to hold a serious conversation. (p. 45, emphasis added)

The critical points in this incisive account are the restrictions on time and atmosphere inherent in the visits a man receives from his wife. Time and atmosphere are precisely the key prerequisites for authentic emotional communication. While absent during regular visits, they are the very qualities that characterize conjugal visits at the Soledad Correctional Training Facility. It will be recalled from the previous chapter that 95 percent of men in the

---

[a]It is interesting to note that federal penitentiaries are generally regarded as having more humane environments and less stringent regulations than do state prisons.

experimental group felt that their visiting facilities (cottages or trailers) were suitable, while this was true of only 20 percent of those in the comparative group, and none of these 20 percent included men who visited in the confined quarters of the protective custody wings. It was also found that the time that a man could spend with his wife during conjugal visits was just about ten times as long as the time made available for ordinary day visits, a factor with obvious consequences for deep and meaningful contact.

It should come as no surprise then that such altogether contrasting visiting experiences should result in significantly different rates of marital stability and, to a lesser extent, parole success as were described in the previous chapter. What is most fascinating about these findings is that they suggest a way to bring about positive change in prisoners, not by subjecting them to a particular treatment of one sort or another, but by providing a homelike atmosphere in which a man can relate to his wife for an extended period of time.

Moos (1975), a psychologist whose special interest is the ecology of social institutions, cites several studies demonstrating markedly lower recidivism rates for juvenile offenders who were confined in smaller correctional settings with a more informal set of rules and regulations. Such work may herald a new and challenging perspective, namely that the environmental determinants of human behavior may be at least as significant as intrapsychic factors in accounting for chronic criminal activities. If further evidence can be marshaled that will corroborate the essential truth of this idea, then the whole notion of "treating" or "rehabilitating" prisoners will have to be overhauled.

To some extent the findings of this research echo the remark of an official at Soledad, who commented casually to this investigator, "We don't rehabilitate anyone. If a man is rehabilitated, he decided to do it for himself." If that is so, then maybe the best thing a penal institution can do to help a prisoner is literally nothing, i.e., do nothing *to* him while simultaneously offering a humane, emotionally nurturing and caring environment *for* him. The 44 hour conjugal visits now available at Soledad offer exactly that kind of environment.

Limitations of this Research

Before the implications of these findings are explored further, it may be useful to outline some of the more significant limitations of this study. While the factors listed below are critical for sound scientific research, they should not be construed as invalidating the definite trends that emerged in the one year followup data. Here then are the constraints which prohibit broad generalizations of the results described above.

1. The *numbers* of subjects in the two samples were relatively small—20 each in the original experimental and comparative groups. Compounding the limitations of these small sample sizes was the fact that, due to circumstances

discussed in the previous chapter, the comparative group ultimately consisted of only 15 men at the time of the followup study. The difficulties that prevented the selection of much larger samples are described in Chapter 3.

2. The time lapse between the "treatment" (conjugal visits) and its inferred effects (family stability and postparole success) was one year. While something of value may be deduced about that period of time, a two to five year followup would have offered more valuable data from the perspective of demonstrating that the effects produced can persist for a longer period of time.

3. It was impossible to ensure that at the time of the followup study all subjects would have been paroled for one full year. Ideally, one would simply have waited until every subject had been released and then examine what happened to each over the course of the next 12 months. However, the necessity of completing the research by a specified date resulted in having to obtain the followup data when 11 men were still imprisoned. For those men, the nature and frequency of disciplinary reports replaced an evaluation of parole problems encountered.

4. The assessment of the status of a couple's marriage is obviously an extremely complicated affair. In the present instance, a separation or divorce were regarded as tangible indices that the marital status had changed dramatically. What was not as clear was the subject's evaluation of the degree of personal adjustment problems he and his wife were experiencing in the relationship. It is conceivable that some men may have represented their marriages as being more satisfying and free of conflict than they actually were. Their wives, after all, were not interviewed, nor were they asked to fill out questionnaires. However, in most cases the parole officers gratuitously included marital information in the forms regarding parole violations. And when they did, it corresponded remarkably well with what the subjects themselves reported about the state of their marriages.

Moral and Legal Issues

Unlike Latin America, where conjugal visits in prison are commonplace (see Chapter 2), in this country such visits give rise to a number of moral and legal questions. The legal issue continues to be fought on the battlegrounds of the state appellate courts of this country. The twin thrusts of the cases are: (1) the contention that the absence of conjugal visits violates the Eighth Amendment's protection against "cruel and unusual punishment" in the form of brutal homosexual rape, and (2) that deprivation of liberty is sufficient punishment for the commission of a felony crime and, consequently, that there is no justification for further denying a man the opportunity to periodically maintain an intimate relationship with his wife. And while on one level this *is* a legal question, it quickly collapses into a moral one, since the law, finally, represents some approximation of a consensual view of how social relations ought to be ordered and circumscribed. Thus, while the courts may issue particular decisions, administrative policy is not likely to alter significantly unless such decisions are seen as right and proper, or their implementation is vigilantly enforced. Neither of these conditions is likely to be realized in the immediate future.

Thus one is compelled to examine whether conjugal visits are something that men in prison deserve to have on a regular basis, or whether it is a special privilege subject to loss if an inmate's behavior does not conform to the standards of custodial authorities. The shortcomings of the view that such visits should be no more than a special privilege are immediately apparent. Holloway (1975) has written of how the loss of conjugal visits at Parchman State Prison in Mississippi has been skillfully used by the staff to intimidate prisoners and to coerce them into acceptable and submissive behavioral routines. But while prison authorities in California are probably less blatantly sadistic than those in Mississippi, the possible use of conjugal visits as an instrument of controlling personal conduct remains a danger in California as well. That this is so is reflected in a recent comment by a San Quentin inmate: "A guy who's got a [family] visit coming up is going to think twice before he gets involved in something. Even if he has a parole date that may be too far off to really mean much. . . the attitude is 'never mind the parole date, but I don't want to lose my visit' " (Newscam, 1976, p. 3).

Such anxieties on the part of prisoners need not exist. The view proposed here is that conjugal visits should be a *right* of all married prisoners and those who have common-law wives, and that they deserve serious consideration for single prisoners whose girlfriends wish to avail themselves of that opportunity. Such a contention can be justified on several possible grounds: (1) conjugal visits are pragmatically beneficial as a means of rehabilitation; (2) conjugal visits promote marital and family stability; and (3) conjugal visits are a human right regardless of any significant change that they do or do not promote in prisoners (comparable in that sense to the right to send and receive mail).

The findings of the present research make a moderate case for the positive effects of conjugal visits on rehabilitation, and an extremely strong case for the positive effects of those visits on marital stability. In the event that further studies reveal strong confirmation of these results, it is likely that many state correctional departments that do not presently have such visits (48 out of 50) would seriously explore the possibility of initiating them. But what if it is shown that the wives and children of prisoners experience clear benefits from conjugal visits, *and* that recidivism is not markedly reduced. Would there then by any rationale for continuing such programs? Indeed there would, and it would rest on the third argument presented above, namely that the right to have adult non-coercive sexual relations is not one that is properly abridged as a consequence of imprisonment.

No one who has studied the history of punishment for criminal acts can fail to appreciate that it has undergone an evolution that (with all of its exceptions) has, as its ideal, the increasingly humane treatment of those who have transgressed society's rules. The use of torture, exile, and mutilation are no longer acceptable in this culture. In addition, we have witnessed the increasing rejection of the demeaning conditions of solitary confinement, gratuitously aggressive behavior on the part of guards, primitive sanitary facilities, and even factors related to the adequacy of food, clothing, and social and medical services in correctional institutions.

What can this movement mean except that we are striving, albeit gradually, toward a new vision of how to deal with criminal offenders? At its heart is the notion that revenge and rehabilitation cannot coexist. If we want only punishment and vengeance, then stark, impoverished environments, stripped of any human touch, will continue to serve us well. If, however, we believe that there may be ways of isolating prisoners in settings that will provide a more humane and caring context than they may have ever before experienced, settings that may or may not affect their future actions, then conjugal visits must be seen as a human right and not as a privilege. In summary, conjugal visits ought to exist, not only because they may be instrumental in producing valuable individual and social benefits, but because making them available is the *right thing to do*— a reflection of justice tempered by mercy.

Obviously citizens incensed by the swelling tide of every type of crime in the United States are not likely to be swayed by the abstract ethical commentary above. They are, however, likely to be affected in their thinking by extensive research that shows that conjugal visits are positively correlated with reduced recidivist rates (especially of less violent crimes) or increased family stability that will reflect itself in decreased welfare rates and juvenile offenses (youngsters without a father are more probable candidates for acts of delinquency than those whose fathers are present and actively involved in their growth and development).

In the context of the circumscribed and not especially life-enhancing atmosphere of most prisons, skepticism regarding the value of a conjugal visiting program is understandable. But as Miller (1969) stated:

In my more optimistic moments, however, I recognize that you do not need complete authority over a social organization in order to reform it. The important thing is not to control the system, but to understand it. Someone who has a valid conception of the system as a whole can often introduce relatively minor changes that have extensive consequences throughout the entire organization. Lacking such a conception, worthwhile innovations may be total failures. (p. 1073)

Thus, the substantive implication of the present research project is that state corrections departments throughout the country should seriously consider the value of initiating conjugal visiting programs, that attendant research should be aimed at determining exactly what consequences such visits have for large numbers of prisoners over several years.[b] Such programs (and their evaluations) are

---

[b]The California Family Visiting Program is an ideal target for such research. According to

likely to strengthen the bonds of family life and to promote social justice, even as prisons themselves are compelled to remain and function primarily as institutions of punishment.

Concluding Reflections on Research Methodology

It would have been sufficient in this study simply to test the two hypotheses and to discuss the implications of the findings. Instead, a major portion of this research effort involved more than 50 hours of probing interviews, intended to elicit detailed information concerning what the experience of a conjugal visit in prison is like for a man and his wife. At first, the aim of the investigator in conducting these interviews was to offer a useful "subjective" supplement to the more "objective" evaluation of the effects of such visits on family stability and parole outcomes. As the study unfolded, however, it became clear that the worth of the collective interviews was certainly equal to the tests of the two hypotheses that had been advanced.

Some of why this is so has been alluded to in a recent paper by Levine (1974):

The logic of experimentation and of statistical inference demands conditions that are difficult, if not impossible to meet in human studies. . . most studies are not and practically speaking cannot be, conducted on the basis of random sampling of the total population. Most subjects are obtained from pools within relatively closed social settings. The people in such settings are uniformly subject to given social forces and to given events. *Even when individuals from such subject populations are randomly assigned to experimental conditions, given that people live within social systems, there is no logical guarantee that some condition which affects all subjects uniformly, a condition unknown and relatively unknowable to the experimenter, is not interacting with the experimental variables to produce the particular set of findings.* (P. 664, emphasis in original)

What this meant in the case of the research at Soledad was that it was impossible to isolate the effects of conjugal visits from the myriad influences of incarceration at South facility (Soledad): i.e., how can one estimate the contribution to ...dings of such factors as the dormitory style housing, the particular ...titute the security staff there, the specific programs available in ... of the prison, etc.? One can't. Therefore, it was thought especially useful to examine not only the consequences of the family visiting program, but

---

the May 1976 issue of the corrections department newsletter, *Newscam*, "the Department has 67 family visiting units. . . both apartments and mobile homes. . . and 30 new units are scheduled to be added in the coming year. . . . During the last quarter of 1976, an estimated 4500 wives, children, parents and other immediate family members poured through the gates of C.D.C. institutions. . . to spend a day or more in surroundings as homelike as staff and inmate talent (and available funds) can provide" (p. 3).

also the subjects' own descriptions of how it altered their psychological reality. Some of the things they speak of as engendered by the visits—hope, caring, intimacy, being touched—are not amenable to mathematical evaluation, but surely that does not diminish the importance to us of knowing about them.

It also became clear to this investigator, during the course of the interviews, that the process of interaction with the subjects was different than what had been anticipated. This became most evident when prisoners identified questions that were irrelevant and others that might be modified in ways that would generate more fruitful information. The research began to assume the dimensions of a reciprocal inquiry; the investigator would frame the structure through suitable scientific lenses and the inmates would clarify issues of content, emphasis, and direction. It began to make more and more sense to treat the subjects as informants rather than as uninformed objects. This research approach has been discussed by Gadlin and Ingle (1975):

This does not mean. . . that we need take our subjects at their word. It does mean, however, developing the means whereby *we can learn from our subjects as well as from their performance.* This particular approach promises a tremendous increase in the information available to us and a new depth to our understanding of psychological events. It also suggests some possibilities for a whole new range of research, in which those we formerly considered our subjects are now our collaborators in research endeavors. Experimentation, when its relational nature is acknowledged, can become a social project rather than a laboratory exercise. (P. 1008, emphasis added)

It was in the light of the statement quoted above that this research was experienced by the investigator as a truly collaborative social project. There was a feeling throughout that "we" might discover something important about how prisons might be humanized, and what there was about conjugal visits that seemed so unique to most of the men who spoke about them. Naturally, the inmates also nurtured the hope that the researcher's presence might lead to the expansion of the extent or frequency of their visits; but when told that the study would quite possibly have no impact on their lives, their desire to participate lost nothing of its original vitality. Perhaps it is time for social scientists to think more and more of facilitating active disclosures from subjects of the shadings of their personal experiences. This may be done within the context of some sort of feedback loop in which a particular method of investigation is constantly subject to revision and modification, based on subject input (as was the case with the text of the protocol used in this study, and the transfer of subjects from the comparative to experimental group).

Psychology as a Means of Promoting Human Welfare

In my opinion scientific psychology is potentially one of the most revolutionary

intellectual enterprises ever conceived by the mind of man. . . . I believe that the
real impact of psychology will be felt, not through the technological products
it places in the hands of powerful men, but through its effects on the public at
large, through a new and different public conception of what is humanly possible
and what is humanly desirable. (Miller, 1969, p. 1063)

This concluding section represents an attempt to explore the relationship between
psychological research on social problems and concerns of value, particularly inso-
far as the nexus between these two may yield clues for a fruitful marriage of the
clinical and research roles of the professional psychologist.

For almost a hundred years now, ever since its birth as a discipline separate
from philosophy, psychology has sought to gain respectability as a science. And
while that has no doubt been an admirable pursuit, it has also raised some very
complicated questions. The physicist or chemist engaged in laboratory research
rarely concerns himself with the political or social implications of his work.
Ideally, his work is done in a value-free context, with the search for truth being
his only measuring rod for success. With the advent of nuclear energy and poison
gases, the luxury of such pristine isolation has no doubt been disrupted. Still,
the old refrain of "We simply discover things. It is for society to decide how to
use or abuse them" is one that is more often accepted than not. Few people
condemn Einstein for his work on making the atom bomb possible as much as
they do Truman for ordering it dropped on Hiroshima.

But the uses of psychological methods and techniques are fraught with difficulties of a normative nature, especially because it is often the psychologist
himself who employs them. The examples of psychosurgery, ECT, behavior
modification, aversive conditioning, and sensory deprivation involve, if not direct
culpability, at least the complicity of the professional psychologist. Those activities are generally employed in institutions such as hospitals, prisons, and mental
health facilities on members of society drawn from the lowest socioeconomic
class.

Given that practices of that sort continued to exist, it is imperative to ask,
as Beit-Hallahmi (1974) does, whether psychologists are conscious of the political context that always surrounds their work. More specifically, do they view
themselves as reflexively serving the interests if those in power, or conversely do
they seek to function as agents of "cultural rebellion"? Choices of that sort
clearly lie in the moral domain.

It is only within the last few years, and mainly since the advent of community psychology, that publications have begun to appear that touch on the
role of the psychologist in doing research on social problems. Statements like
the one below illustrate the extent to which some thinkers believe that psychologists influence the *Weltanschauung* of our time:

There are no absolute truths in the social sciences, where the "facts" are embedded in a particular theoretical framework which in turn rests upon certain

epistemic and metaphysical presuppositions. In short there is an intimate relationship between statements of value and statements of fact . . . psychologists
[must become] more self-conscious of the implications of their research with
respect to creating a specific image of man and society . . . by formulating a
specific conception of man and his nature, prescription leads to a specific kind
of description and knowledge. In this way values and social science are inti-
mately interlocked, and this interdependent relationship must be made explicit
and understood within psychology to the extent that psychology does, should,
and hopes to participate in the creation of a better society. (Buss, 1975, p. 991)

It is difficult to imagine any natural scientist agreeing with comments of
this sort as guiding principles of the scientific enterprise. And perhaps that is
just as well. It may be that the unique distinction of psychology may turn on
its potential for using the scientific method for the acquisition of knowledge
while necessarily finding itself enmeshed in questions of value. And if that is
psychology's destiny, it may become the first systematic activity of man
designed, consciously, to further the ends of human evolution. That would
mean the fostering, by psychology, of those conditions that maximize material,
emotional, intellectual, and spiritual freedom for all human beings on the
planet.

It may well be asked what possible relevance such lofty goals have to the
conducting of psychological research. Tyler (1973) touches on the issue by
presenting what she refers to as a "design for a hopeful psychology." In it she
states: "It is my conviction that many if not most research undertakings can
be planned so that they will contribute both to our storehouse of general
knowledge and to the improvement of human individuals and their society"
(p. 1025). She recalls, not sentimentally, but rather with the passion borne of
commitment, some graduate students choosing to study psychology "at least
partly as a hope that the science of human behavior will eventually make
possible a better society, one in which exploitation and coercion will be
replaced by more humane and effective ways of handling the business of the
human race. Some of us can still remember the hopes we held for human progress when we first decided to become psychologists" (p. 1021).

These comments derive from an earlier theme discussed by the author,
that of a triadic intersection of considerations that are thought critical prior
to undertaking any research project in psychology. These she itemizes as (1)
the potential contribution to an organized body of knowledge, (2) the potential
value for the subjects who participate in the research, and (3) the potential contribution to society (p. 1025).

It is hoped that this book is an example of that kind of research. And that
will be so if the following objectives will have been at least partially realized:

1. a description has been provided of the severe psychological and social
damage that result from sexual deprivation in prison;

2. subjects interviewed have conveyed either the special worth to them
of conjugal visits or the frustrating constraints of regular visits;

3. the California Department of Corrections, by realizing the potential value of the family visiting program, will expand it to include maximum and protective custody inmates, and will provide a budgetary allotment that allows for increasing the number of trailers and cottages at each state prison. In addition, the experience in California may provoke other state correction departments to initiate conjugal visiting programs in the near future.

One last concern remains to be discussed. Its significance is most forcefully addressed in a seminal paper by Caplan and Nelson (1973) that has not yet received the attention it so richly deserves. The article, entitled "On Being Useful: The Nature and Consequences of Psychological Research on Social Problems," contains more than can be adequately dealt with here. But its importance warrants at least a cursory glance at the main thread of its argument. The central thrust of the authors' theme is expressed in this statement: "Whether the social problem to be attacked is delinquency, mental health, drug abuse, unemployment, ghetto riots, or whatever, the significance of the defining process is the same: *the action (or inaction) taken will depend largely on whether causes are seen as residing within individuals or in the environment*" (p. 201, emphasis in original).

It is this motif of person versus situation-centered blame or causality that is at the heart of how psychologists conceptualize and approach the amelioration of social problems. The point is made that the organization and presuppositions of much behavioral science research has too often resulted in "blaming the people in difficult situations for their own predicament" (p. 202).

An example of the contrasting analyses that may be brought to bear on a social problem is suggested by the issue of juvenile delinquency. A person-centered definition would emphasize such factors as the inability to delay gratification and the incomplete sexual identity of young offenders. It would imply treatment strategies in the form of counseling, behavioral shaping, or coercive measures. By contrast, a situation or environment-oriented perspective would stress the substitution for criminal paths of alternative opportunities to achieve socially valued goals. That way of viewing the problem would imply some form of system change in the form of efforts to create suitable occasions for teenagers to experience the tangible fruits of success and accomplishment through the use of their own efforts and imagination. From this point of view the target for change is the social or economic arrangements of a particular community or society rather than the psyches of individual young people who are designated as "bad."

The authors observe that there are specific reasons that account for the traditional focus by psychologists on person-oriented factors. The most transparently obvious is that it is in the nature of their discipline to study individuals and their mental states—thoughts, attitudes, motives, and intrapsychic dynamics. They contend that "when it comes to the actual study of . . . man and why he behaves as he does, we are more likely to limit our search for etiological evidence to what goes on between his ears and to ignore or exclude from consideration a multitude of external impingements that could justifiably be hypothesized as causal." (p. 202).

But it is not simply the person-centered research approach per se that bears questioning in this regard, but *which* persons get studied. Social scientists are keenly aware that the realization of professional advancement is not enhanced by helping people who are without power. Hence one may notice that:

certain groups within society become continually stigmatized as problem groups (e.g., migratory workers, mental patients, blacks, the poor) because they are visible and accessible, but most especially, because they are vulnerable to the social scientist for research purposes. . . .Nonachieving lower income children are more identifiable and accessible as a research population than are greedy "entrepreneurially motivated" slumlords...there is a lack of data on landlords, bankers, and city officials who permit building code violations that would justify using *them* as targets for person-change treatment efforts. (p. 207)

Criminals, of course, are a prime target for the person-oriented bias in studying social problems. This has had the predictable result of social scientists devising scores of "treatment" programs designed to change them into respectable middle class citizens. The provision of conjugal visits is radical in this context, because instead of trying to stimulate change it "merely" attempts to conserve what is already of value in a man's life.

Caplan and Nelson also perform a long-needed analysis of the political functions of individual-biased interpretations of social problems. They astutely observe that such research often serves as a convenient apology for absolving the government and social institutions from any responsibility for the problem's existence. Consequently, the locus of ameliorative action will be on "treating" the victims rather than on an analysis of the structural defects of particular social systems. Looking at social problems in that fashion also reinforces favorite American myths of the Horatio Alger genre that contend that each individual is the master of his own fate. Subscribers to this myopic view of social reality may then be guiltlessly complacent about those who have not "made it on their own."

What all of this results in is a self-congratulatory preservation of the status quo. In completing their line of thought the authors proffer the following bit of wisdom: "The sooner we recognize that [social science] knowledge is not truth divorced from the realities of time, place, or *use*, the better will be our chances of making a truly responsible contribution to societal improvement" (p. 211).

If this study even begins to raise questions as to the ways in which professional psychologists may utilize research as a means of promoting human welfare, it will have succeeded well enough. But a final note of caution is in order for those who would take up the cause of the disadvantaged, the powerless, and the oppressed:

There is no solution to the value problem that will settle the issue once and for all, no answer that will show the way to a condition of man which is free of conflict. We must settle for a path of progress, for progression as a process, for a direction rather than an end. The path of progress is clear....It formulates no final goal; the mastery of one problem is followed simply by undertaking the next. But it defines a path that leads away from humbug and ignorance and exploitation and toward understanding, control, and freedom. (Wheelis, 1958, p. 205)

Interview with Administrative Staff at Soledad Correctional Training Facility

In an effort to gain some historical perspective and administrative overview of the family visiting program, several key staff persons were interviewed. These included Mr. Tom Stone, superintendent of the Soledad Correctional Training Facility; Mr. E. A. Peterson, associate superintendent (and chief administrative officer of South facility, where most of the research took place); Lieutenant Derral Byers, former coordinator of the family visiting program at South; and Ms. Leah Bradshaw, correctional counselor and present coordinator of the program at South.

All interviews took place on July 24, 1975.

Interviewer: What was the department of corrections' objective in starting the family visiting program?

Stone: Back in 1968, Procunier (former director of corrections) asked Superintendent Lloyd down at Tehachapi to experiment with it. It went off with less trouble than anyone expected though only minimum custody inmates were allowed to participate.

Peterson: The main objective was to bring families together prior to release. At first, down at Tehachapi, an inmate had to be within 90 days of his release date to qualify. In addition, he had to show that he had specific plans regarding his intentions after he left the institution.

Interviewer: How did the family visiting program at Soledad get started?

Stone: The trial program at Tehachapi showed that it could work. When I arrived here in 1971 about 5 percent of the inmate population had such visits. At that time a man had to have minimum custody status and be within six months of his parole date. That meant he'd already been separated from his family for several years in many cases. Now 90 percent of the men in this institution are eligible—all except those in protective custody and maximum custody. Also, since it is not always feasible to bring the prisoner *out*, the next best thing seemed to bring the family *in*. I had visited Mexico and seen the facilities they had there for conjugal visits. But I didn't like the idea of such visits taking place in a man's cell.

Interviewer: Do you think it would be valuable to provide voluntary counseling to a man and his wife as part of the family visiting program, especially near the end of his sentence, as a means of easing the inevitable period of adjustment after release?

This interview is reprinted by permission.

Stone: I have reservations about that. It would be a much more valuable thing to offer *after* parole. My experience is that most men are in a somewhat unreal state just before their departure.

Byers: It's available through counselors and chaplains, but seldom used.

Interviewer: Could you comment on the historical objections offered by penal administrators as to why conjugal visits are not feasible—security difficulties, budgetary considerations, space, community attitude, embarrassment to wife, cheapens sexuality, discriminates against single men, etc. Are any of these legitimate to you or do you see them essentially as rationalizations for inaction?

Stone: Look, it scared hell out of me at the beginning, especially in terms of security factors, but we wanted to do it and we did.

Peterson: Well, there was some concern from the community and a spurt of letters to the editor of the local newspaper. However, we were very specific in pointing out that it was family visits, not conjugal visits that we were initiating.

Byers: Yes, there are money problems. The program, as it exists now, is not financially supported by the state. Funds for its operations are taken from other line budget items plus donations. And as far as security goes, the problems can be considerably minimized by good classification.

Bradshaw: I see those reasons essentially as rationalizations.

Interviewer: What kind of feedback, if any, have you had from the surrounding community regarding the family visiting program? What is the best way to convey the value of such a program to the public?

Peterson: Well, the reactions have been mixed. The best way to educate people is through outside contacts with interested public-spirited citizens like the speaking engagements of my community awareness group which includes inmates participating in the family visiting program. In addition we've sponsored tours of our facility for outside groups in order for them to see how different the men in here are from what their notions of them might be.

Interviewer: Have you had any communications from inmates' wives concerning their attitudes about the family visits?

Stone: Yes, and they've all been extremely positive.

Peterson: Many of the wives say it's the best thing that ever happened. One, who's married to an inmate who had been an alcoholic prior to coming to prison said that the visits enabled them to talk clearly and honestly for the first time.

Bradshaw: Yes, it's been positive, except that some of the wives of medium custody inmates have been concerned about the time gap between visits [about once every three months].

Interviewer: On the basis of its existence so far, what would you say are the most significant benefits realized by the family visiting program?

Stone: First, it gives the man an important relationship to hang on to. Another by-product is that staff-inmate relations have improved. The "do this, do that" mentality has changed as officers have met the wives and children of many of the men.

Peterson: It seems to have stabilized marriages and humanized the attitude of the staff.

Byers: There has been a tendency to forestall separation and divorce.

Bradshaw: It's an important approximation of normality.

Interviewer: Have you had any negative comments about the program from men not eligible to participate, such as single men and men with common-law wives?

Peterson: A few complaints, but mainly the men are glad to see that others have it.

Byers: No.

Bradshaw: No.

Interviewer: Could you compare the value of the family visits as opposed to having furloughs in terms of promoting marital and family stability?

Stone: Furloughs may also be valuable, but their liability is that they are only available near the end of a man's sentence.

Bradshaw: Family visits are much more frequent over a longer time period. Furloughs are temporary and occur mainly at the end of a sentence and are particularly available to men who have had stable family situations anyway.

Interviewer: Can a man in prison marry in order to become eligible for family visits if he's lived for some time with a common-law wife?

Stone: Yes, they can legally be married in the prison chapel and we've had about a hundred men who've done just that.

Byers: Yes; the main purpose is to give the kids legal parents and the wife a semblance of stability. They must have lived together for at least two years and have that confirmed by nonfamily members of the community.[a]

Interviewer: Is there any procedure available for transferring men who are married to other institutions so that wives will not be plagued by distance and financial problems in order to participate in the program?

Peterson: We try to do it, but it's difficult. The largest concentration of wives are in the southern part of the state.

Bradshaw: Not based on the issue of family visits alone. Other reasons would be necessary in order to effect a transfer.

Interviewer: Is a man eligible for family visits immediately after arriving at the institution?

Peterson: He's eligible 90 days after his arrival in accordance with the present calendar of scheduled visits.

---

[a]Since the date of this interview this has changed. At the present time prisoners can now get married without having had a previous common-law relationship with the intended bride.

Interviewer: Is there any factor other than limitations on present facilities that determines the frequency of family visits? Theoretically, if you had as many trailers as you wanted, would every married man be able to have visits monthly?

Peterson: Yes, the number of apartments and trailers is the only factor affecting the frequency of such visits.

Interviewer: I understand you've requested additional trailers and personnel in order to expand the family visiting program. What changes would occur if you were granted everything you requested?

Stone: The most extensive program in the institution would be family visiting. It would be three times as large as it is currently.

Peterson: Every inmate who was eligible would be able to have visits every four to six weeks.

Interviewer: Do you have any impressions as to whether the regular involvement of a man in family visits has any significant impact on postparole success?

Stone: I believe it does, and hope that you're the one who'll find out whether that's so.

Peterson: Certainly. I don't see regular participants coming back to prison.

Bradshaw: We have no figures on it, but I'd guess that it does.

Interviewer: As it exists now, family visiting is a privilege. Does this mean that the staff can use such visits as an instrument of control, that is, threaten to take away family visits if a man doesn't behave himself? And do you think it ought to be a right rather than a privilege?

Stone: For minor infractions family visits are not affected. For those of a serious nature a man may lose them.[b]

Peterson: I believe it should be a privilege. We don't want to reward bad behavior.

Byers: As an administrator I always look for ways of controlling a man's behavior. Having rights would do away with such means of control.

Bradshaw: I consider it a privilege. I'm not sure it should be a right. If it were we would have no leverage in terms of affecting behavior.

Interviewer: Do you think family visits should be available to unmarried inmates who have had a steady relationship with a common-law wife or girlfriend for some relatively long period of time?

Stone: I'm in favor of their being available to common-law wives.

Peterson: I would have no objection.

Byers: No, I suppose I'm from the old school. If you open it up in that way the public will have additional ammunition against its existence.

---

[b]Officials at Soledad state that this policy has changed since the date of the interview so that "men now are not restricted from family visits because of poor disciplinary record unless the infractions are directly related to visiting or family visiting."

Bradshaw: Essentially yes, if the relationship can be demonstrated to be an enduring one.

Interviewer: Why aren't the men in protective custody and close custody allowed family visits?

Stone: Only in order to guarantee their own safety in the case of the men in protective custody.

Peterson: There's some justifiable fear that they would be subject to attack, the men in protective custody that is, because of gang warfare, or having "snitched" etc. But we're trying to get a separate location for them that might enable even those men to have family visits.

Byers: With the maximum custody men there's the possibility of escape, and the fact that often such men have been caught with contraband.

Interviewer: What do you think accounts for officers' comments about "going to the boneyard" and other suggestive remarks reflecting a belief that a man's sole interest during such visits is sexual in nature?

Peterson: That phrase actually came from the inmates and the officers picked up on it. Initially officers resented the program. Gradually some old-timers retired and others saw that the program had value in changing behavior and making the job a little easier.

Byers: They do tend to see it as only a sexual thing. There's a reluctance to see its broader implications except in the case of younger officers. Older ones still tend to bad-mouth it.

Interviewer: How would you compare the value of the family visits with the ordinary visits?

Stone: While regular visiting is vital in its own way, family visits are much more effective in retaining family relationships, not only with wives but also with parents, children, and brothers and sisters.

Peterson: The physical intimacy is a significant difference. Also the ability to sit down and share food together.

Byers: There's no comparison. Two uninterrupted days in a trailer is a totally different experience.

Bradshaw: Family visits are a lot more valuable. It's a whole different atmosphere—an opportunity for privacy and for the inmate to assume a parental role with respect to his children.

Interviewer: What has been the attitude of your professional colleagues in the field of corrections from other states to the family visiting program?

Peterson: They're apprehensive and curious. Several have asked questions about how it got started, and especially about fiscal and security problems.

Byers: I've had little professional contact of that sort. But the ones who have communicated with me have been amazed. The general nature of their comments is "Boy, you give convicts everything out there."

Interviewer: Do you think there's any program available at Soledad that has as much value as the family visiting program?

Peterson: None.

Byers: No.

Bradshaw: Probably not. There could be if the possibility of therapy were offered.

Interviewer: What do you think the future holds for family visits in terms of its expansion here in California and its increasing adoption by other state prison systems?

Stone: It's probable that other states will begin similar programs because of learning of California's success.

Byers: I think eventually it'll spread to the other states.

Interviewer: Is there anything else you'd like to add concerning your feelings about the nature and worth of the family visiting program?

Peterson: Its present success is leading to an expansion. Funds are the critical factor.

Bradshaw: It entails lots of complicated administrative problems and inmate complaints about scheduling and so on, but none of it would justify cutting or limiting it. It's just too valuable.

Byers: I had a thousand families to deal with. It broadened my understanding of people.

Appendix B

The Family Visiting and Regular Visiting Questionnaires

Family Visiting Program Questionnaire—Soledad Correctional Facility

Interview # _____   Date of Interview_____

1. How often do you receive visits from your wife?
   About every _____weeks.

2. How many visits have you had from your wife altogether? _____.
   During what period of time? _____

3. Do you find the cottage/trailer a suitable place for a family visit in terms of privacy and comfort?
   Yes _____ No _____ If not, why not?

4. Do you find that inmates using the cottage/trailer leave it neat and clean for the next man and his family to use?
   Yes _____ No _____

5. Complete the following statements: The 44 hour visit seems to last _____ hours/days to me.

6. Given the limitations of facilities and the number of men desiring family visits do you find two days a relatively sufficient time for such visits?
   Yes _____ No _____ If not, what amount of time would be sufficient? _____

7. Describe any thoughts, fellings, or fantasies you may have the day *before* your wife visits; the day *after*.
   Before:

   After:

8. If you have children, does your wife bring them with her when she visits?
   Yes _____ No _____ N.A. _____ If yes, how often; if not, why not?

9. If your children do visit, do they ever comment on their feelings regarding your imprisonment?

10. Does your wife bring you any special food that you like which is not available (or in limited quantities) as part of the prison diet?

11. Does your wife generally seem comfortable or ill at ease during the visits?
    Comfortable _____ Ill at ease _____ If ill at ease do you know why?

12. Do you discuss the frustrations and difficulties of prison life with your wife?
    Yes _____ No _____ If so, how does she react? If not, why not?

115

13. What kinds of family matters do you discuss most with your wife?
    a. your marriage _____   d. future plans _____
    b. children _____   e. other _____
    c. money _____

14. Does your wife experience any travel difficulties, physically or financially, in order to visit you?
Yes _____ No _____ If so, what kind of difficulty, and does it affect how often she visits you?

15. Sex is obviously a very important factor in the family visits. Is there anything that is as important or more important to you during these visits?
Yes _____ No _____ If so, what?

16. The time gap between visits is relatively long. Does this lead to any sexual anxiety or difficulty on your part when the visiting takes place?
Yes _____ No _____ If so, do you know why?

17. Is your wife as sexually comfortable and responsive during the visits as she is at home?
Yes _____ No _____

18. Do you enjoy sex more, less, or the same during family visits than in your own home?
More _____ Less _____ Same _____ If more or less, how come?

19. Have you ever asked your wife whether she has had any extramarital affairs while you've been in prison?
Yes _____ No _____ If yes, her response? If not, why not?

20. Do you think the family visiting program discriminates against single inmates?
Yes _____ No _____ If yes, how so?

21. Do you think common-law wives and girlfriends ought to be allowed family visits with inmates?
    Common-law wives   Yes _____ No _____
    Girlfriends   Yes _____ No _____

22. Family visits like those in California exist in no other state. What do you think is the corrections department's purpose in allowing such visits?
    a. stabilize marital relationship _____
    b. help decrease homosexuality _____
    c. increase control over prisoners _____

23. What is the most important benefit you receive from the family visiting program?

24. Is there any program available to you here in Soledad which is as valuable to you as the family visiting program?
Yes _____ No _____ If so, what?

Descriptive Data:

Name _____

How long married? _____ Number of children _____

Ethnic background: White _____ Black _____ Asian _____ Hispanic _____

Age _____

Place of birth _____

Present offense _____

Number of previous offenses _____

Total time in prison this conviction _____ all others _____

Time left before parole _____

Regular (Ordinary) Visiting Questionnaire—Soledad
Correctional Training Facility

Interview # _____   Date of Interview _____

1. How often do you receive visits from your wife?
    About every _____days/weeks.

2. How many visits have you had from your wife altogether? _____
    During what period of time? _____

3. Do you find the area set aside for visits suitable in terms of privacy and comfort?
    Yes _____ No _____ If not, why not?

4. How long do your visits with your wife usually last? _____

5. How long does the visit *seem* to last? _____

6. Do you find the amount of time allotted for visits sufficient?
    Yes _____ No _____ If not, what would be sufficient?

7. Describe any thoughts, feelings, or fantasies you may have the day *before* your
    wife visits; the day *after*.

8. If you have children, does your wife bring them with her when she visits?
    Yes _____ No _____ N.A. _____ If yes, how often; if not, why not?

9. If your children do visit, do they ever comment on their feelings regarding your
    imprisonment?

10. Does your wife generally seem comfortable or ill at ease during the visits?
    Comfortable _____ Ill at ease _____ If ill at ease, do you know why?

11. Do you discuss the frustrations and difficulties of prison life with your wife?
    Yes _____ No _____ If so, how does she react; if not, why not?

12. What kinds of family matters do you discuss most with your wife during visits?
    a. your marriage _____   d. future plans _____
    b. children _____   e. other _____
    c. money _____

13. Does your wife experience any travel difficulties, physically or financially, in
    order to visit you?
    Yes _____ No _____ If so, what kind of difficulty, and does it affect how often
    she visits you?

14. Have you ever asked your wife whether she has had any extramarital affairs while
    you've been in prison?
    Yes _____ No _____ If yes, her response?; if not, why not?

15. Family visits like those in California exist in no other state. What do you think is the correction department's purpose in allowing such visits?
   a. stabilize marital relationships _____
   b. help decrease homosexuality _____
   c. increase control over prisoners _____

16. What is the most important benefit you receive from being able to receive visits from your wife?

Descriptive Data:

Name_____

How long married? _____ Number of children _____

Ethnic background: White _____ Black _____ Asian _____ Hispanic _____

Age _____

Place of birth _____

Present offense _____

Number of previous offenses _____

Total time in prison this conviction _____ all others _____

Time left before parole _____

Appendix C

One-Year Followup Study Forms

Form 1: Family Visiting Program Postrelease Questionnaire

To: _____

    Please indicate for the parole information data that is most accurate for
_____up to the present time:

_____ a. *No Parole Difficulties:* no arrests or violations.

_____ b. *Minor Parole Difficulties:* arrest without conviction, fine, absconded from
supervision.

_____ c. *Serious Parole Difficulties:* new felony conviction or return to prison as a
result of parole violation.

    Please describe in a few sentences the specific details of the category checked
above:

How long has this individual been on parole?

Form 2: Family Visiting Program Followup Marital
Status Questionnaire

To: _____

   Last year I interviewed you at Soledad with regard to your participation in the
family visiting program. Now I am doing a one year followup study which is as
important as that initial contact with you. I am asking you to take a *few minutes* of
your time to fill in the answers to the questionnaire below. Your honest and direct
responses will be very much appreciated. Thank you in advance for your cooperation.

Followup Data

1.   Please indicate your current marital status:

     Married _____

     Separated _____ If so, how long? _____

     Divorced _____ If so, how long? _____

2.   Which of the following statements best describes your marriage at the present
     time?

     _____ a. Basically satisfactory; minimal problems.

     _____ b. Moderate conflicts which are being handled to our satisfaction.

     _____ c. Major conflicts causing severe stress to the marriage.

     _____ d. Problems serious enough so that there is a good chance we will
                  separate and/or divorce in the near future.

Form 3:   Followup Data on Family Visiting Project —
Men Not Paroled

1.   Would you please check the statement which most accurately represents inmate
     _____ 's behavior from *May 1975* until
     present time (i.e., for the past 12 month period).

     _____ a.   No disciplinary infractions — inmate's behavior has been appropriate
                    for this institution.

     _____ b.   Minor disciplinary infractions.

     _____ c.   Major disciplinary infractions.

2.   If you checked (b) or (c) to question 1 above, would you indicate below the
     number and *nature* of the infractions involved.

\
_____
Signature and title.

References

Allen, T. Psychiatric Observations on an Adolescent Inmate Social System and Culture. *Psychiatry,* 1969 *32* (3), 292-302.

American Friends Service Committee. *Struggle for Justice: A Report on Crime and Punishment in America.* New York: Hill & Wang, 1971.

Bagdikian, B. *The Shame of Prisons.* New York: Pocket Books, 1972.

Bakan, D. *On Method: Toward a Reconstruction of Psychological Investigation.* San Francisco: Jossey-Bass, 1967.

_____. The Mystery-Mastery Complex in Contemporary Psychology. *American Psychologist,* 1965, *20* (2), 186-91.

Balough, J.K. Conjugal Visitations in Prison: A Sociological Perspective. *Federal Probation,* 1964, *28* (3), 52-58.

Barnes, H.E. & Teeters, N. *New Horizons in Criminology.* New Jersey: Prentice-Hall, 1959.

Beit-Hallahmi, B. Salvation and Its Vicissitudes: Clinical Psychology and Political Values. *American Psychologist,* 1974, *29* (2), 124-29.

Berkey, B. Psychiatric Sequelae of Sexual Deprivation. *Medical Aspects of Sexuality,* 1971, *5* (10), 176-84.

Boring, E.G. The Nature and History of Experimental Control. *American Journal of Psychology,* 1954, *67,* 573-89.

Braswell, M. & DeFrancis, P. Conjugal Visitation: A Feasibility Study. *Georgia J. of Corrections,* 1972, *1* (4), 171-80.

Brodsky, S.L. *Families & Friends of Men in Prison.* Lexington, Mass.: D.C. Heath and Co., 1975.

Buffum, P. *Homosexuality in Prisons.* Washington, D.C.: U.S. Department of Justice, 1971.

Buss, A. The Emerging Field of the Sociology of Psychological Knowledge. *American Psychologist,* 1975, *30* (10), 988-1002.

California Department of Corrections. *Family Visiting.* Sacramento, Ca.: 1972.

Caplan, N. & Nelson, S.C. On Being Useful: The Nature and Consequences of Psychological Research on Social Problems. *American Psychologist,* 1973, *28* (3), 199-211.

Cartwright, D., ed. *Field Theory in the Social Sciences: Selected Theoretical Papers by Kurt Lewin.* New York: Harper and Bros., 1951.

Cavan, R. & Zemans, E. Marital Relationships of Prisoners in Twenty-Eight Countries. *J. of Criminology, Law & Police Science,* July-August 1958, pp. 133-39.

Chaiklin, H. Integrating Correctional and Family Systems. *American Journal of Orthopsychiatry,* 1972, *42* (5), 784-91.

Chaneles, S. The Open Prison. *Psychology Today,* March 1975, pp. 9-15.

_____, *The Open Prison.* New York: Dial Press, 1973.

Clark, R. *Crime in America.* New York: Pocket Books, 1974.

Clemmer, D. *The Prison Community.* New York: Holt, Rinehart & Winston, 1965.

_____. Some Aspects of Sexual Behavior in the Prison Community. *Proceedings of the American Correctional Association,* 1958, 374-82.

Cohen, S. & Taylor, L. *Psychological Survival—The Experience of Long Term Confinement.* New York: Vintage, 1974.

Coleman, L. Toward the Divorce of Psychiatry and Law. *Virginia Law Quarterly,* 1974, *27* (10). Reprint.

_____. Prisons: The Crime of Treatment. *Psychiatric Opinion,* 1972, *9* (5), 5-16.

Conjugal Visits in Prison Hailed. *New York Times,* August 15, 1967, p. 26.

Conrad, J.P. *Crime and Its Correction: An International Survey of Attitudes and Practices.* Berkeley, CA.: University of California Press, 1970.

Cressey, D., ed. *The Prison: Studies in Institutional Organization and Change.* New York: Holt, Rinehart & Winston, 1961.

Crowell, Collier & MacMillan. *International Encyclopedia of the Social Sciences,* 1968, *9,* 267-71.

Danziger, P. Sexual Assaults and Forced Homosexual Relationships in Prison: Cruel and Unusual Punishment. *Albany Law Review,* 1971, *36* (2), 428-38.

Davis, A. *Report on Sexual Assaults in the Philadelphia Prison System and Sheriff's Vans.* Philadelphia: District Attorney's Office, 1968.

Debs, E. V. *Walls and Bars.* Chicago: Charles Kerr and Co., 1927.

Eckartsberg, R.V. An Approach to Experiential Social Psychology. In A. Giorgi, W.F. Fischer, & R.V. Eckartsberg, eds., *Phenomenological Psychology.* Vol. 1. Pittsburgh: Duquesne University Press, 1971.

Faith, K., ed. *Soledad Prison: University of the Poor.* Palo Alto: Science and Behavior Books, 1975.

Fenton, N. *The Prisoner's Family.* Palo Alto: Pacific Books, 1959.

Fishman, J. *Sex in Prison.* New York: National Library Press, 1934.

Fortune News. "Prison Sexuality." New York, April 1974. Pp. 2-5.

Gadlin, H. & Ingle, G. Through the One-Way Mirror: The Limits of Experimental Self-Reflection. *American Psychologist,* 1975, *30* (10), 1005-12.

Gagnon, J. & Simon, W. The Social Meaning of Prison Homosexuality. *Federal Probation,* 1968, *32* (1), 23-29.

Galtung, J. The Social Functions of a Prison. *Social Problems,* 1958, *6* (2), 130-41.

Giorgi, A. The Experience of the Subject as a Source of Data in a Psychological Experiment. In A. Giorgi, W.F. Fischer, & R.V. Eckartsberg, eds. *Phenomenological Psychology.* Vol. 1. Pittsburgh: Duquesne University Press, 1971b.

_____. Phenomenology and Experimental Psychology. In A. Giorgi, W.F. Fischer, & R.V. Eckartsberg, eds., *Phenomenological Psychology.* Vol. 1. Pittsburgh: Duquesne University Press, 1971a.

Glaser, D. *The Effectiveness of a Prison Parole System.* New York: Bobbs-Merrill, 1964.

Haggerty, J. *Sex in Prison.* New York: Ace Books, 1975.

Haynor, N. Attitudes Toward Conjugal Visits for Prisoners. *Federal Probation,* 1972, *36* (1), 43-49.

Holloway, H.X. Sex at Parchman: Conjugal Visiting at the Mississippi State Penitentiary. *New England Law Review,* 1975, *10* (1), 143-55.

Holt, N. *California's Pre-Release Furlough Program for State Prisoners.* Sacramento: Department of Corrections Research Division, 1969.

Holt, N. & Miller, D. *Explorations in Inmate-Family Relations.* Sacramento: Department of Corrections Research Division, 1972.

Hopper, C. Sexual Adjustment in Prisons. *Police,* 1971, 75-77.

_____. Conjugal and Family Visitation in Mississippi. *Proceedings of the American Correctional Association,* 1969b, 257-64.

_____. *Sex in Prison: The Mississippi Experiment with Conjugal Visiting.* Baton Rouge: Louisiana State University Press, 1969a.

Howlett, J. Marital Deprivations of Prisoners and Their Wives. *Prison Service Journal,* 1973, *12,* 6-7.

Ibrahim, A. I. Deviant Sexual Behavior in Men's Prisons. *Crime and Delinquency,* 1974, *20* (1), 39-45.

Irwin, J. *The Felon.* Englewood Cliffs: Prentice-Hall, 1970.

Johns, D.R. Alternatives to Conjugal Visiting. *Federal Probation,* 1971, *35* (1), 48-52.

Karpman, B. Sex Life in Prison. *J. of Criminal Law, Criminology & Police Science,* 1948, *38* (5), 475-86.

Kassebaum, G. Sex in Prison. *Sexual Behavior,* 1972, 2 (1), 39-45.

Kelman, A. *A Time to Speak: On Human Values and Social Research.* San Francisco: Jossey-Bass, 1968.

Killinger, G. & Cromwell, P., eds. *Penology: The Evolution of Corrections in America.* St. Paul: West Publishing Co., 1973.

Kinsey, A.C.; Pomeroy, W.B.; & Martin, C.E. *Sexual Behavior in the Human Male.* Philadelphia: Saunders, 1948.

Lamott, K. *Chronicles of San Quentin.* New York: Ballantine Books, 1972. Used with permission.

Leinwand, G. *Prisons.* New York: Pocket Books, 1972.

Levine, M. Scientific Method and the Adversary Model: Some Preliminary Thoughts. *American Psychologist,* 1974, *29* (9), 661-77.

Levy, H. & Miller, D. *Going to Jail.* New York: Grove Press, 1971. Used with permission.

Lewin, K., ed. *Studies in Authority and Frustration.* Iowa City: University of Iowa Press, 1944.

Lindner, R. Sexual Behavior in Penal Institutions. In Deutsch, A. *Sex Habits of American Men.* New York: Prentice-Hall, 1948.

Lloyd, G.P. A Family Visiting Program for Offenders in Custody. *Medical and Biological Illustration,* 1969, *19* (3), 142-46.

Markley, C. Furlough Programs and Conjugal Visiting in Adults Correctional Institutions. *Federal Probation,* 1972, *36* (1), 19-26.

Martin, J.B. *Break Down the Walls.* New York: Ballantine Books, 1951.

Masters, W.H. & Johnson, V.E. *Human Sexual Response,* Boston: Little, Brown & Company, 1966.

McConnell, J. Criminals Can Be Brainwashed—Now. *Psychology Today,* April 1970, pp. 74-75. Used by permission.

McGuire, W. Some Impending Reorientations in Social Psychology: Some Thoughts Provoked by Kenneth Ring. *Journal of Experimental Social Psychology,* 1967, *3,* 124-36. Used by permission.

Miller, G.A. Psychology as a Means of Promoting Human Welfare. *American Psychologist,* 1969, *24* (12), 1063-75.

Mitford, J. *Kind & Usual Punishment: The Prison Business.* New York: Vintage Books, 1974.

Moos, R.H. *The Human Context: Environmental Determinants of Behavior.* New York: Wiley Interscience, 1975.

Morris, N. *The Future of Imprisonment.* Chicago: University of Chicago Press, 1974.

Morris, P. *Prisoners and Their Families.* New York: Hart Publishing Co., 1965.

Murphy, G. The Courts Look at Prisoners Rights. *Criminology,* 1973, *10* (4), 441-569.

National Council on Crime and Delinquency. A Model Act for the Protection of the Rights of Prisoners. *Crime and Delinquency,* 1972, *18* (1), 27-29.

Neese, R. *Prison Exposures.* New York: Chilton Press, 1959.

Nelson, V. *Prison Days and Nights.* Boston: Little Brown, 1932.

Newscam (California Department of Corrections Newsletter), May 24, 1976.

New York Times, August 15, 1967, p. 26. Used by permission.

Nussbaum, A. The Rehabilitation Myth. *American Scholar,* 1971, *40* (4), 674-75.

Ohlin, L.E. The Stability and Validity of Parole Experience Tables. Doctoral dissertation, University of Chicago, 1954. *Dissertation Abstracts International.* 1954.

Orne, M. On the Social Psychology of the Psychological Experiment: With Particular Reference to Demand Characteristics and Their Implications. *American Psychologist,* 1962, *17,* 778-83.

Rausch, H.L. & Willems, E.P. *Naturalistic Viewpoints in Psychological Research.* New York: Holt, Rinehart, and Winston, 1969.

Rieger, W. A Proposal for a Trial of Family Therapy and Conjugal Visits in Prison. *American Journal of Orthopsychiatry,* 1973, *43* (1), 117-22.

Ring, K. Experimental Social Psychology: Some Sober Questions About Some Frivolous Values. *Journal of Experimental Social Psychology,* 1967, *3,* 113-23.

Roth, L. Territoriality and Homosexuality in a Male Prison Population. *American Journal of Orthopsychiatry,* 1971, *41* (3), 509-14.

Sanford, N. Will Psychologists Study Human Problems? *American Psychologist,* 1965, *20,* 192-202.

Scudder, K. *Prisoners are People.* New York: Doubleday, 1952.

Selltiz, C. et al. *Research Methods in Social Relations.* New York: Holt, Rinehart and Winston, 1961.

Shaw, G.B. *The Crime of Imprisonment.* New York: Greenwood Press, 1946.

Sheldon, R. Rehabilitation Programs in Prison. *Psychiatric Opinion,* 1972, *9* (5), 17-21. Used by permission.

Silber, D.E. Controversy Concerning the Criminal Justice System and Its Implications for the Role of Mental Health Workers. *American Psychologist,* 1974, *29* (4), 239-44.

Sobell, M. *On Doing Time.* New York: Charles Scribner's Sons, 1974.

Soledad Correctional Training Facility Memorandum, May 23, 1975.

Stuart v. *Heard.* 359 Federal Supplement 921 Texas, U.S. District Court S.D. June 1973.

Sykes, G. *The Society of Captives.* Princeton University Press, 1958.

Thomas, P. *Seven Long Times.* New York: Praeger Publications, 1974.

Torok, L. *The Strange World of Prison.* New York: Bobbs-Merrill, 1973.

Tyler, L.E. Design for a Hopeful Psychology. *American Psychologist,* 1973, *28* (12), 1021-29.

Vedder, C. & Kind, P. *Problems of Homosexuality in Corrections.* Chicago: Charles Thomas, 1965.

Ward, D. Inmate Rights and Prison Reform in Sweden and Denmark. *Journal of Criminal Law, Criminology and Police Science,* 1972, *63* (2), 224-31.

Weinberg, K. Aspects of the Prison's Social Structure. *American Journal of Sociology,* 1942, *47* (5), 717-26.

Weiss, C. & Friar, D.J. *Terror in the Prisons: Homosexual Rape and Why Society Condones It.* New York: Bobbs-Merrill, 1974.

Westin, A.F. *Privacy and Freedom.* London: Bodley Head, 1970.

Wheelis, A. *The Quest for Identity.* New York: W.W. Norton and Co., 1958.

Willems, E. & Rausch, H., eds. *Naturalistic Viewpoints in Psychological Research.* New York: Holt, Rinehart, and Winston, 1969. Used by permission.

Williams, E.Y. & Elder, Z. The Psychological Aspects of the Crimes of Imprisoned Husbands on Their Families. *Journal of National Medical Association,* 1970, *62* (3), 208-12.

Yee, M. *The Melancholy History of Soledad Prison.* New York: Harper's Magazine Press, 1970.

Zemans, E. & Cavan, R. Marital Relationships of Prisoners. *Journal of Criminal Law, Criminology and Police Science,* 1958, *49* (1), 50-57.

Index

Index

About the Author

Jules Quentin Burstein is Associate Director of Buckelew House, a residential treatment facility for schizophrenics in Kentfield, California. He also maintains a private practice in marriage and family counseling in San Francisco, and is a contract instructor at the California School of Professional Psychology. Previously he was an assistant professor at City University of New York under whose auspices he worked at the Queens County Jail, establishing and administering educational and counseling programs. He is the author of *General Mathematical Ability* (Cowles Book Co., 1971) and has also published articles in *California Living* and the *Village Voice*. His degrees include the B.A. in mathematics from Brooklyn College, the M.A. in philosophy from New York University, the M.A. in psychology from the Graduate Faculty of the New School for Social Research, and the Ph.D. in clinical-community psychology from the California School of Professional Psychology.